CRITICAL THINKING: HELPING STUDENTS LEARN REFLECTIVELY

S. SAMUEL SHERMIS
PURDUE UNIVERSITY

 CLEARINGHOUSE ON READING AND COMMUNICATION SKILLS

 PRESS

1992

Published 1992 by:
ERIC Clearinghouse on Reading and Communication Skills
Carl B. Smith, Director
2805 East 10th Street, Suite 150
Bloomington, Indiana 47408-2698
and
EDINFO Press

ERIC (an acronym for Educational Resources Information Center) is a national network of 16 clearinghouses, each of which is responsible for building the ERIC database by identifying and abstracting various educational resources, including research reports, curriculum guides, conference papers, journal articles, and government reports. The Clearinghouse on Reading and Communication Skills (ERIC/RCS) collects educational information specifically related to reading, English, journalism, speech, and theater at all levels. ERIC/RCS also covers interdisciplinary areas, such as media studies, reading and writing technology, mass communication, language arts, critical thinking, literature, and many aspects of literacy.

This publication was prepared with funding from the Office of Educational Research and Improvement, U.S. Department of Education, under contract no. RI88062001. Contractors undertaking such projects under government sponsorship are encouraged to express freely their judgment in professional and technical matters. Points of view or opinions, however, do not necessarily represent the official view or opinions of the Office of Educational Research and Improvement.

The photo of John Dewey was taken at his summer retreat on Sawlor Lake, Hubbards, Nova Scotia. It was used with permission from Special Collections, Morris Library, Southern Illinois University at Carbondale.

Library of Congress Cataloging-in-Publication Data

Shermis, S. Samuel
    Critical thinking : helping students learn reflectively / by S. Samuel Shermis.
       p.   cm.
    Includes bibliographical references (p.79–87).
    ISBN 0-927516-28-4
    1. Critical thinking—Study and teaching.   2. Thought and thinking—Study and teaching.   I. ERIC Clearinghouse on Reading and Communication Skills.   II. Title.
LB1590.3.S48 1992
370.15'2—dc20   91–44698
                                              CIP

TABLE OF CONTENTS

SOCRATES

L.P. Boitard Fecit.

Why We Still Do Not Teach Reflective Inquiry

Throughout the 20th century, a persistent criticism has been directed against American schools: Students must learn to become more thoughtful about what they learn. In place of either indoctrination in allegedly mainstream cultural values or memorization, students need to learn to become critical thinkers, to develop the skills of problem-solving, to learn to inquire. The rationale for this position has scarcely varied over the years:

1. The requirements of a political democracy are that its citizens must become autonomous decision-makers.

2. The extremely rapid social change that arose during the Industrial Revolution fomented social problems without parallel in world history. To prevent our society from self-destructing requires that individuals learn the skills of problem-solving.

3. The imperative that all children are to develop their potential requires that they become adults who have learned to think meaningfully about themselves and their world.

4. Insights from the social and behavioral sciences, especially psychology, suggest that learning is best when individual learners develop insight, and learning is purposive.

Expressed in these terms, who would be opposed to reflective thinking? Why would anyone resist teaching students to be active, careful thinkers who habitually search for support and anticipate consequences? Why would anyone reject the notion that learning should be purposive and goal-oriented? An answer to these questions might suggest explanations as to why America's public schools, despite educators' lip-service to the great John Dewey, have failed to incorporate the recommendations of America's foremost philospher of education throughout all subjects and in all grades!

BARRIERS TO REFLECTIVE INQUIRY

Unless teachers understand the forces that stand in the way of conducting reflective inquiry in schools, even the most well-disposed teacher will likely be unsuccessful at teaching critical thinking. Teachers who adopt assumptions that run counter to critical inquiry will be unable to promote reflective thinking, critical thinking, and problem-solving. These assumptions—most of which are held without conscious awareness—will block attempts to teach students to think in an independent fashion.

Who and what are the obstacles to critical thinking? One set of obstacles I label "philosophical," notions that were first codified and described in Athens in the fourth century B.C.E. The second set of obstacles I call "cultural," referring to patterns of behavior in American culture that depress attempts at critical thinking.

WHAT PHILOSOPHICAL ASSUMPTIONS PREVENT REFLECTIVE THOUGHT?

Numerous philosophical propositions underlie the large body of assumptions that guides our educational practice. Many of these philosophical assumptions are unrecognized, held without awareness. Too many of these philosophical propositions interfere with reflective inquiry. Siegel and Carey discussed notions of meaning that come from what philosophers call a "naively realistic" view of the world. (Siegel and Carey, 1989) I have analyzed other philosophical assumptions in educational foundations which appear to be barriers to reflective inquiry (Shermis, 1967), as have also Ernest E. Bayles (Bayles, 1950, 1960) and John Wynne (1963). The following are examples of some of these philosophical assumptions so unhelpful to critical reflection:

- ❖ Reality has an objective existence only; it lies outside of us and has nothing to do with our perceptions.

- ❖ When reality has been apprehended properly, the result is *knowledge.*

- ❖ True and valid knowledge has already been discovered and reduced to atomistic blocks or bite-sized pieces. Textbooks contain knowledge that is verified and therefore valid.

- ❖ Meaning, likewise, is something that people acquire by discovering what is "out there."

- ❖ Learning consists of apprehending this external, completely objective reality found in textbooks, known by teachers, and prescribed by syllabuses and curriculum guides.

- ❖ Thought is one thing and action is another, just as theory is one thing and practice another. These *dualisms* pervade the world; they are eternally opposed to one another and cannot be reconciled.

- ❖ Critical thinking is a matter of identifying specific skills and teaching them in separate exercises. (Siegel and Carey, 1989)

Some assumptions have been described by educational psychologists, most prominently Morris Bigge (Bigge, 1976; Bigge and Hunt; Wynne, 1963):

> *Before one can think, one must first acquire a certain minimal amount of basic information. This notion—which has the status of revealed truth—is based upon a conception of mind that has been demonstrated to be invalid since the late 19th century. However, it is widely held by many teachers and liberal arts professors and is known as "mind substance," that is, the mind consists of a thing.* (Bigge, 1976)

One conception of mind substance is *mind as vessel*, into which information is poured and from which it is retrieved later. Another conception is *mind as muscle*, according to which the various components of the mind can be exercised and developed, much as the various muscles of the body can be exercised and developed. This conception became a part of *faculty psychology*; in the 19th century, many psychologists and teachers had inherited the belief that the mind could be subdivided into many separate fundamental constituent elements called "faculties." In Western civilization it has been thought that certain subject matters are appropriate for each faculty, and that these develop the mind from latent potential to actual functioning capacity. Thus, Latin grammar and history would develop the faculty of memory, music would develop the faculty of appreciation, and geometry would develop the faculty of logic. Once developed, the various faculties would enable automatic transfer of thought. That is, when an individual developed the faculty of logic through mathematics, he or she would then be habitually logical.

Given these premises, education has been defined largely as a process of developing separate faculties.

Knowledge can be phrased as propositions that are either true or false.

Truth can be determined by correspondence with what an authority—teacher, textbook, syllabus, curriculum-maker—has stated.

In a parallel development, humans were seen as complex mechanisms that can be *conditioned* to make proper *responses*. In our society at the turn of the century, an entire educational theory with accompanying teaching strategies evolved under the leadership of Edward Lee Thorndike. Later, this position was further developed by B. F. Skinner. (Skinner, 1976) From a Thorndikian, *stimulus/response* position, education is properly conceived as shaping responses through presentation of proper stimuli. From a Skinnerian position, a "schedule of reinforcements" *reinforces* the proper behavior. According to this conception, the teacher is the active shaper, and the students become so much clay. Given this conception of teaching—which has been thoroughly institutionalized in public schools—reflective inquiry is a logical impossibility. Indeed, any notion that individuals can autonomously develop purposes, and inquire in response to them, is, argued Skinner, a vestige of the pre-scientific ages of "perfectionistic or utopian thinking." (Skinner, 1976)

Effects of all of these conceptions, if not the conceptions themselves, are firmly entrenched; they are held both by professional educators and by the general public as well. Many of them are taken to be self-evidently valid; without being consciously identified, they are often employed by laypersons. (Wynne, 1963) For instance, the conception of mind as a kind of substance has made intuitive sense to parents and coaches who believe that participating in sports will promote both strong muscles and an attitude known as "good sportsmanship." It can easily be demonstrated that tennis, football, and vigorous exercise improve muscle tone and cardiovascular functioning, but many also believe that attitudes learned while playing team sports *automatically* transfer to other situations. Thus, developing grace under pressure, not whining or losing one's temper, cheerfully congratulating the winner, learning cooperation and teamwork, and abiding by both written and unwritten "rules of the game," are thought to carry over into life beyond the playing field. This "mental discipline" approach, a type of faculty psychology, has been adopted by most Americans on the assumption that competitive athletics develops a latent faculty of good sportsmanship which, once learned on the playing field, will carry over to all the rest of life.

In terms of the experimental evidence, however, there is not the slightest evidence that there is *necessary* transfer of attitudes from the playing field to the job, home, civic organization, or anywhere else. By the same token, as William James, Edward Lee Thorndike, and Robert S. Woodsworth demonstrated nearly a century ago, just as memorizing nonsense syllables does not improve the "faculty" of memory, there is no reason to believe that studying particular subjects will improve other faculties, or that playing team sports will make one ethical. (Hilgard, 1948; Bigge and Hunt, 1968; Bigge, 1976) There is no experimental evidence that geometry necessarily improves one's ability to reason properly, that memorizing the *Preamble* induces patriotism, or that conjugating Latin and Greek verbs improves character—although these arguments have been, and are still, used widely. In fact, these notions of faculty psychology form the assumptions behind a good many recent, widely publicized national reports on education.

TEACHING AS TRANSMISSION

The implication of these philosophical assumptions taken together is the almost universal conception of *teaching as transmission*. Consider the interconnected set of beliefs that most teachers employ: Knowledge consists of so many inert things—usually called "facts"—which are organized in containers called "textbooks," and dispensed by transmitters, considered authoritative, called "teachers." Most members of our culture uncritically accept the notion that *what is taught in schools has an inherent validity of its own*, for example, that reading, arithmetic, the definition of "peninsula," and the Periodic Table of Elements are inherently important and are, furthermore, *necessary for survival in the conceivable future*. Unfortunately, because students often do not appreciate the significance of these subjects, concepts, or skills, they usually lack motivation to learn them; they must therefore be "motivated"—driven, coerced, bribed, rewarded, and punished—into learning them.

Another example of *mind as vessel* is *mind as storage vault*. Whereas teachers often candidly acknowledge that memorizing the minutiae of civics may not be useful *now*, they usually argue that it will come into service when the student grows up to become a citizen. The actual outworking of this assumption is the Magruder series of civics textbooks, published since 1917, a thick compendium of disconnected bits of information on elections, the Constitution, taxes, laws, and other political trivia, which are memorized, almost immediately forgotten, and have not been demonstrated to play any apparent part in actual civic behavior. Grammar texts—unconnected with actual reading, writing, or speaking—from which students were required to memorize the names of parts of speech and grammatical rules, are another example of stored lore that has little connection either with good writing or anything else. Biology texts, similarly, which featured thousands of bits of terminology and the Linnean taxonomy, were designed to improve the faculty of memory. This did not happen, however, nor did students learn from them very much about scientific thought, scientific phenomena, or the scientific component of social problems.

In the last decade, politicians, teachers, and the public have persuaded themselves that nationally administered, standardized tests provide an excellent index of how well students are learning. While nationally standardized tests have been around since the early 1920s, they have assumed extraordinary importance in the latest episode of pointing with alarm at American public schooling. High scores on SATs and other instruments are thought to signify good learning; low grades are believed to indicate that Hispanic, Black and Native American children are doing poorly. The pervasiveness of low test scores has functioned as a rationale for such "reforms" as lengthening the school year, requiring more courses in mathematics and science, and toughening standards. It has also provided yet another basis for teachers to continue drill-and-memory-level testing. Teachers frequently lament the tests, maintaining that the need to get high scores on nationwide tests is the reason that they avoid teaching high-level thinking or studying a topic in any depth. Nationwide tests, then, are blamed for drill, routine, and *memoriter* learning.

This, however, appears to be a rationalization, a convenient excuse. In fact, teachers were emphasizing drill, routine, and memorization long before such tests were institutionalized in the early 1920s. It is arguable that even without such tests, teachers would continue the traditional assign/read-text/recite/test-on-text pattern of teaching. Tests, then and now, provide a convenient scapegoat for ignoring the imperative to teach critical thinking.

Over many years of supervising student teachers, I have learned of another scapegoat. It is called "the community." Teachers have stated that they would love to deal with interesting issues, but that "the community *expects* me to cover the curriculum." To the question, "Has any member of the community actually told you that he or she *expects* you to cover transitive verbs and Jacksonian Populism?" the answer invariably comes back:

"Well, not in so many words...." My next question is, "Then, why do you feel that the community is united in expecting coverage of particular concepts?"

The answer is, "This expectation is transmitted through the *principal.*" My analysis is that whether the community and/or the principal really articulates a demand for specific content coverage, is really not the issue. These expectations as *perceived* by administrators and teachers, take on the status of reality. I argue that the practice of detailed, systematic coverage at the Bloom-I level flows out of teachers'—and ultimately out of our society's—conception of mind as reservoir.

PHILOSOPHICAL ABSOLUTES

Another philosophical barrier to reflective thinking and teaching lies in the 2,500-year-long history of absolute ideals coming to us from Athenian society. While Platonic and Aristotelian thought differ in important respects, both of those two great Greeks accepted the existence of philosophical absolutes. An absolute in philosophical terms is that which exists at all times and in all places. (Shermis, 1967; Bayles, 1960) It exists on its own terms. It exists whether it is known or not. An absolute carries its own imperative: Because the absolute exists, humans must come into the proper relationship with it. This has come to mean that the function of teachers is to acquaint students with the nature of given absolutes. For Aristotle, this meant that once one understood the *essence* of a given entity, one understood it for all time. Other philosophers have employed various absolutes to justify inculcation of assorted concepts.

As a result of these perduring Greek philosophical assumptions, certain logical consequences pervade educational practices in American schools. Despite objections of thoughtful educators who since the second decade of the 20th century have relentlessly deplored these practices, educational absolutism has, perversely, achieved cultural sanction. Some of these practices—such as defining teaching as transmission, assuming that the "mind" exists only to be filled or exercised, and making the textbook synonymous with the curriculum—have defeated all attempts thus far to introduce critical thought. Why has this been the case? What is there about these assumptions and practices that preclude critical thought and reflective inquiry?

A NON-ABSOLUTE SET OF PHILOSOPHICAL ASSUMPTIONS FOR REFLECTIVE THINKING

Reflecting, thinking, and teaching are thoroughgoingly relativist, and therefore they are non-absolutist. (Bayles, 1966; Bigge, 1971) The argument, however, is not that there is no absolute reality, but that the only reality that humans can know is what they interpret of the world around them. All of us interpret sounds, visual objects, material things, immaterial concepts, and the like. What I make of the world around me constitutes my reality, and the same goes for you. When we put our perceptions together, and negotiate agreement about the world, it is called the "social construction of reality."

This argument is no academic quibble. If meaning involves an interaction between a person and his or her world, then there is no meaning *out there*, waiting to be known on its own terms. Teaching, consequently, is neither a matter of a teacher's requiring students to come into the proper relationship with an absolute ideal, nor a matter of having students latch onto the "right" value.

Why ought an advocate of critical thinking reject the absolutist position? First, the assumptions of absolutism are unexamined premises, held unconsciously. They function as the beginning of a deductive process, and they are used to reach conclusions; because the assumptions on which this process goes forward are unexamined, the product of thought is undisciplined, random, and disconnected. Thinking like this fails because it is not controlled by reference to a goal.

Second, absolutist ideals have supported the largely self-defeating notion of curriculum as a collection of concepts organized and arranged as subject-matter experts have organized them. Textbooks embody this conception. They continue the practice begun in colonial America of using catechisms, hymnals, psalters, and the Bible as texts. (Bayles and Hood, 1966) Because the Bible was held to be the revealed word of God, and therefore inerrant, every word in it was literally true. The student's function was to receive the absolute written truth. Until 1860, furthermore, Calvinist theology dominated colonial education. (Bayles and Hood, 1966; Best and Sidwell, 1967; Button and Provezano, 1989) Three Protestant convictions permeated education: Humans are saved by faith alone; the Bible is the source of faith; literacy is needed for comprehension of the Bible. What began in colonial America as an outgrowth of theological convictions ended up as the practice of treating *all* texts as if they, too, were inerrant, an expression of objective truth, and essential to be learned on their absolute terms.

Textbooks are taken by absolute-minded teachers to be the only source of valid data, which puts them above criticism; they are authorities to be received and memorized. No inquiry and questioning are invited.

In practice, it has proved impossible both to *receive* and at the same time to *inquire* into textual statements. Research evidence in classrooms supports the notion that most teachers do not promote criticism of textbook content. Indeed, the lack of critical thinking in classrooms, the tendency to ask memory-level questions, and the practice of "covering the material" systematically have been researched for many years. (DeBoers, Kaulfers, and Metcalf, 1966; Hunt and Metcalf, 1968; Kurfiss, 1988; Raths, Wassermann, Jonas and Rothstein, 1967; Stanley; Shaver, Helburn and Davis, 1978) If the most important operational educational goal is to transmit a certain amount of information in a certain time period, then it is at the same time logically impossible to raise questions about that material or pursue the questions to answers that differ from the answers "in the book." The self-imposed requirement of teachers to cover ground, indoctrinate culturally approved values, and discipline students' minds, have thwarted critical thinking for over two centuries.

Memory-level questioning, expository lectures, textbook domination, ritual and routine, have been built into school systems since the 1770s. At that time, the first large American educational bureaucracy was born in Boston. (Schultz, 1973) The Board of Education then was dominated by merchants, businessmen, and factory owners. Looking for a model for their schools, they copied factory organization, architecture, and administrative structure. Moreover, they borrowed from the state-supported education system in Prussia, with its heavy emphasis on top-down control and allegedly rationally organized bureaucracies. The students in the schools, like the workers in the factories, furthermore, were to be submissive and docile workers who would happily accept their destiny as factory hands. (Spring, 1988, 1989; Apple, 1988) In its search for something to supplant the haphazard, erratic, and disorganized curriculum of schools at the time, the Boston school committee believed that factory organization would supply uniformity.

The factory organization of schools was implemented in the 19th century when "professional," male administrators; age-grading (Hutchings and Shermis, 1991); text-dominated curriculum; and curriculum driven by low-level concepts became institutionalized in the American public-school system. By the end of the 19th century, socially marginal teachers—often poorly paid young women—and a male-dominant administrative hierarchy became the status quo. Except for the attacks of a few radical critics, this pattern has remained unchallenged into the ninth decade of this century. (Katz, 1975; Pratte,1979, 1983; Goodman, 1960; Karrier, 1973; Spring, 1988, 1989; Freire, 1985) If *all* curriculum is to be found in a textbook and can be reduced to propositions that are either true or false, then reflective inquiry, which is based upon the assumption that knowledge and meaning are constructed, and that data may come from a variety of sources, is not a logical possibility. Statements that are either true or false cannot possibly raise problems or become the "anomalies" recommended by Nielsen as starting points for inquiry. (Nielsen, 1989, pp. 15-16) If the most important goal of administrators is to make certain that their students show up well on standardized tests, the better to please the community, and if teachers perceive that this is indeed the school's primary goal, they will then proceed to teach "to the test" throughout the entire semester. One result is that neither the time nor opportunity is made for inquiry.

When I argue that these practices have received cultural sanction for many, many years, this should be interpreted to mean that they are *normative*. Therefore, most students can pass from kindergarten to graduate school, and never have been exposed to any alternative model of teaching or learning. In fact, evidence collected since 1912 demonstrates that from kindergarten to graduate school, most teachers, most of the time, ask questions designed to elicit "correct responses" and "right answers." (Hunkins, 1971) When asking in-class questions, end-of-chapter questions, or test questions, teachers tend to confine themselves to the first two levels of Bloom's taxonomy. (Brannen, 1973; Allen, 1979) Thus, while many teachers are undoubtedly sincere in their desire to encourage students to think, they typically have had few, if any, models in their experience who exemplified open-ended, inquiry-oriented, critical thinking. *Teachers tend to teach as they have been taught. Thus, despite the thin veneer acquired in methods classes in teacher-education programs, most teachers lack philosophical assumptions relevant to, and teaching strategies consistent with, an inquiry approach to teaching and learning.*

Public education constitutes a system with many interconnected, interactive components. Systems theory has demonstrated that to change a single component of a system sends ripple effects throughout all components of the system. (Millstein and Belasco, 1973) In the somewhat forbidding language of systems theory, "The fifth universal systems property is that all systems have factors that affect the structure and function of the system." (Immegart and Pilecki, 1973) Hence, it is not possible to change a single component without concern for the rest of the system because the desired change may be inconsistent with expectations and purposes built into the system as a whole. Therefore, whereas the desire to introduce thoughtful, problem-solving education in American schools had been clearly articulated even before 1915 and 1916 (Barnard, 1915; Dunn, 1916), this desire has remained unfulfilled because no one is willing to ripple the system. Schools that have been set up for the purpose of transmitting what is assumed to be mainstream American cultural values have, so far, resisted the efforts of those few who have hoped in vain to introduce a critical view of the students' social world.

Training in critical thought and the capacity to inquire have not found a home in American public schools.

I am not the first to make these observations; they have been made frequently. Why have schools so successfully blocked all attempts to introduce reflective inquiry in classrooms? It is essential that those who wish to make reforms in public schools inquire into the reasons for this successful resistance to most reform efforts in the schools.

Teachers habituated to the comfortable routine of assign / lecture-and-recite / read-textbook / multiple-choice-examination may prefer not to make the required effort to achieve an essential change. To a teacher who has been teaching for many years by employing the transmission approach, no self-evident reason recommends itself as a compelling motivation to depart from normative teaching practices.

Teachers who may be fearful of engaging in discussions in which ready-made clear answers are missing, may also be reluctant to lose their status as authority figures. The Office for Intellectual Freedom of the American Library Association and the American Civil Liberties Union have argued that teachers fearful of upsetting the community will quite deliberately avoid dealing with whatever they perceive to be controversial. Because what is controversial, unclear, and at issue is precisely that which stimulates thinking, the deliberate exclusion by communities and teachers of critical reflection tends to perpetuate a bland curriculum, one which upsets no one but is as exciting as a bowl of tepid milk.

Therefore, while virtually no one intentionally opposes reflective thinking in principle, certain conventions, traditions, and unverbalized anxieties have thus far prevented reflective thinking and teaching from taking hold in schools.

EVALUATION

Teachers' questions and doubts about reflective teaching and thinking can be reduced to the following question: How would we evaluate student learning? To this question about assessment, I offer the following answers:

1) Assessment of critical thinking and reflective inquiry does not proceed through typical objective questions because they tend to require memory-level responses (Level One on the Bloom Taxonomy, see Appendix) or, at the most, Comprehension (Bloom Level II).

2) Making evaluations in a reflective teaching situation ought to cause a teacher to assess students' ability to think critically. This involves a wide variety of sub-skills, e.g., identifying discrepancies, recognizing problems, being able to phrase testable statements, finding and using data that are both adequate and relevant, supporting assertions, making proper inferences from given statements, and qualifying conclusions.

3) Evaluations can take a good many forms in addition to a paper-and-pencil test: oral reports, written reports, classroom discussion, debates, panel discussions, group projects, and original productions such as a one-act play. Essay exams are an excellent means of assessment, but they are largely neglected because of two erroneous beliefs: that they take "too much time" to grade and that "objective" tests are more accurate and less biased.

The first error stems from ignoring the amount of time it requires to devise, edit, and type multiple-choice, fill-in, completion, true-false, and similar test questions. Because computers can grade many exams rapidly, it is easy to forget how much time is required to prepare an objective test.

The second error, or oversimplification, raises a complex philosophic problem. What exactly is meant by "objectivity?" After all, some human teacher or curriculum specialist must make judgments about 1) what is worthy of being known and tested, 2) how to phrase a test question, 3) what constitutes a "correct" answer, and 4) how to interpret students' answers. In light of these observations, in what sense are objective tests objective, i.e., free from bias and subjectivity?

With practice, teachers can learn to write essay questions that are relatively unambiguous and which actually test higher cognitive levels, such as analysis, synthesis, and evaluation

(Bloom Levels IV, V and VI). The requirement of any evaluation of reflective thinking is that teachers must devise criteria by which to make—and defend—judgments. No absolute or definitive set of criteria exists by which to test the results of reflective teaching. Teachers must devise their own evaluation procedures, and these are guided by their aims, insights, skill, and experience. Some broad but useful criteria might include the following:

1. The student product must deal adequately with the issue; it must answer the question.

2. It must deal with as much evidence as is obtainable, given the usual restrictions.

3. Supportive facts, evidence, concepts, and assertions must be present and accurate.

4. If the evaluation involves essays, reports, etc., all statements must be consistent or harmonious. Self-contradictions, or statements which lead in opposite directions, are not permitted without explanation.

5. Whatever is presented must be done in a literate manner. Essays for which time allows rewrites need to be free from confusing syntax, bad spelling, and awkward or clumsy usage. In-class essays can be "quick and dirty." Verbal presentations must be comprehensible. Correct form is an outward expression of mental order.

Other criteria are certainly possible. What counts is that a teacher expends thought and effort to set up a rational standard of judgment. Without rational criteria, teachers seem to be arbitrary in their grading. Students resent capricious judgments which, then, are defeating for everyone.

A SEMANTIC ANALYSIS

Two of my colleagues and I tried to analyze the failure of reflective inquiry in American schools. (Barr, Barth, and Shermis, 1977) Following our analysis of what we called "the semantic problem," we argued that the *terminology* of reflective inquiry—understanding, critical thinking, preparation of future citizens for rapid social change, creativity, analysis, problem-solving, and decision-making—has triumphed. Teachers employ these terms, and they can all be found in textbooks, newspaper editorials, syllabuses, and professional and popular publications alike. Indeed, teachers frequently use these words to describe what they do in their classrooms. Thus, when a critic calls for problem-solving, teachers agree sincerely and say, "Yes, and I do it; my class is studying problems." I recall talking with a high-school history teacher who told me that his class was studying "the problems that Roosevelt faced in 1932," but this teacher was oblivious to the lack of perception by everyone in his classroom, himself included, that Roosevelt's problems in 1932 were in any way a problem for themselves here and now.

The terminology and concepts that John Dewey used in some of his major works (e.g., *School and Society, How We Think, Democracy and Education*) have won acceptance among educators. Dewey's language with regard to drill, instruction, needs, and growth was quoted approvingly already in the 1916 report (Dunn, 1916), and has even been cited in subsequent sources. Such terms as "problem" and "problem-solving"—as well as all the variants and modifications of these concepts—are still widely used today, although Dewey is not identified as the source. In short, Dewey's *language* triumphed, and very few educational texts omit discussion of "problems," "problem-solving," "democracy," "growth," the school as a laboratory for testing ideas, and the like. However, Dewey's *philosophy* has not—despite claims to the contrary—gained acceptance. What appears to have happened is that educators relabeled in Deweyan language what they had been doing all along. Thus, the after-the-chapter *questions* became after-the-chapter *problems*. In the 1960s and 1970s, authors of numerous curricula (e.g., the New Social Studies, Biological Sciences Study Curriculum, ChemStudy) claimed that their products were organized around a problem-solving rationale.

The problems on which these curricula were focused, however, were the problems that various scholarly disciplines entertain, those topics and themes which delight the minds of astronomers, anthropologists, historians, and biologists

(Shermis, Barth, 1978), but these problems were not necessarily the ones that students would have identified as either problematic or interesting. In fact, many of the so-called problems were as abstract and remote as the curricula they were designed to replace. Nonetheless, they were called "*problems*," and their inventors claimed that they were following a problem-solving rationale. They did indeed employ a model of problem-solving, but it was not one that began with the concerns, issues, and problems that students typically raise. The language of Dewey had been appropriated but not his spirit.

School teachers and university professors have gained a superficial acquaintance with Dewey's terminology without reflecting upon the implications of the terms. That most critical term "problem" is usually employed without awareness that this word can refer to at least these five things:

1. after-the-chapter questions which are in effect problem *exercises*

2. the themes that structure the inquiry of a scholarly discipline, i.e., *disciplinary* problems

3. *social* problems

4. *policy* problems, i.e., difficulties that a society experiences in deciding how to cope with a social problem, such as poverty or drug abuse

5. *inquiry* problems, designated by Dewey as those which demand that an individual actively reflect upon whatever has caused a settled matter to become unsettled (Shermis and Barth, 1983)

All these are labeled "problems," but a problem exercise, which is nothing more than an after-the-chapter question, has little to do with an inquiry problem.

A good example of an inquiry problem that invaded many schools was precipitated by the 1990 war in the Persian Gulf. The public began buying maps of the Middle East as fast as they could be published. Americans who would not have been able to locate Iran, Iraq, Israel, Saudi Arabia, and Kuwait on a map a few months earlier if their lives depended on it, suddenly acquired geographical sophistication. The paradox here is that geography has been a staple of citizenship education for a century and a half. Most of us had been exposed to instruction about geographical placenames, but former students who perfunctorily filled out workbooks on geographical locations went on only to forget immediately what they had memorized unwillingly. A probable explanation for this is that junior-high geography teachers answered questions that no one ever raised. Now, however, we were speaking about the historical origins of Middle Eastern countries after World War I as well as the strategic and military importance of the Kuwaiti-Iraqi border. Because a life-and-death problem had fallen on the world in August, 1990, geographical knowledge had suddenly gained great significance and utility. This is what I mean by "problem": When someone else's problem becomes *your* problem and *mine*, then we get serious in our reflective inquiry concerning it.

ECLECTICISM

Another factor in the difficulty of promoting reflective thought is that Americans tend to accept an *eclectic* approach to any matter. Our culture tends to emphasize flexibility, experimentation, and pragmatic accommodation; therefore, little blame attaches to logical contradiction and theoretical inconsistency. Thus, teachers see no difficulty in accepting the proposition that it is possible to cover text chapters systematically by asking low-level questions and administering objective test items *and also* teach reflectively. No logical conflict is perceived! Taking a hodge-podge approach, teachers simply do not sense their inconsistency. In America, consistent and systematic theory is not very high on most priority lists, especially that of melting-pot schools.

Reflective inquiry requires a considerable amount of theoretical sophistication, but this is precisely what teachers have tended to avoid. This admittedly unflattering and negative judgment can be understood by referring to Philip Jackson's findings that teachers tend to be atheoretical, to ignore the content of their professional training, to disdain theory, to act intuitively most of the time, and to base their decisions on what "feels" comfortable. In Jackson's words, "[Teachers tend to lack] a technical vocabulary, skimming the intellectual surface of the problems they encounter, fenced in, as it were, by the walls of their concrete experience...." Teachers, continues Jackson, do not question the order of things:

> Interest in educational change was usually mild and typically was restricted to ideas about how to rearrange her room or how to regroup her students—how to work better with the educational "givens," in other words. This acceptance of the educational status quo, which might be described as a kind of pedagogical conservatism, appeared to be part of the general myopia typifying the classroom teacher's intellectual vision. (Jackson, 1968, p. 148)

What is the problem inherent in refusing to think theoretically about teaching? All who recommend some form of critical thinking have emphasized that intellectual activity is essential for both teachers and students. All have emphasized such theoretical activities as the search for fruitful problems, their translation into intelligible terms, the quest for meaning, the development of a tolerance for ambiguity, the imperative need to cultivate an attitude of skepticism, awareness of *levels* of validity and *degrees* of truth, the necessity to engage in prolonged analysis, as well as the equally important requirement to consult the perceptions of children, and the need to devise accurate instruments of evaluation. All of this requires a high degree of sustained thought.

But the typical teachers' opinion of "theory" is that it is "ivory-tower speculation" distantly related to the daily classroom routine. That *theory* can refer to a body of abstract ideas that give direction to practical activity, is far removed from most teachers' thinking. That is to say, critical thought requires teachers to engage in theorizing; and without teachers' willingness to entertain a theoretical basis for classroom practices, reflective inquiry is not going to happen.

In sum, because of socialization to norms of thought that derive originally from Athenian philosophy of the fourth century B. C. E., both the wider public and the teaching profession have built up perceptions, attitudes, practices, and institutions that have effectively precluded all attempts to institute reflective inquiry.

CULTURAL FORCES

Other forces that lie beyond, and apart from, life in schools impinge on what happens in schools. These forces have been called "cultural," which is the anthropological term that means "the ways of behaving found in the society." Some of these forces, easily overlooked, tend to defeat efforts to teach reflective thought in schools.

ECONOMIC FORCES

For over 35 years, economist John Kenneth Galbraith has written on the same set of themes describing a complex process of consumerism according to which members of our culture must be trained to devour that which is produced by ever more efficient factories. Galbraith has explained the development of three economic practices that are designed to persuade consumers to purchase and consume the products of a technology grown so efficient that it has reversed the traditional assumption about production and consumption, to wit, that production would *never* catch up with the needs and wants of consumers. This, according to Galbraith, is no longer the case, so our culture has developed advertising as an expertly crafted, almost totally pervasive, strategy designed to promote enthusiastic, if thoughtless, consumption. In addition, easy credit, product obsolescence, and yearly style changes all function to make consumer goods appear outdated and passé, all in order to induce individuals to go into debt in order to buy what is irresistibly new and probably not needed. (Galbraith, 1958, 1967)

When we juxtapose the ethos of consumerism with the demands of critical inquiry, we see that these manufacturing and distributing practices tend to defeat what has been verbally endorsed as the major function of schools in our democratic society, namely, to train critical thinkers. Were young persons trained to be truly critical consumers, they might not be so easily gulled into buying, rapidly using up, discarding, and buying again. If our populace were to reject unthinking consumerism, the economic effects might be disastrous.

Another interesting example of the conflictual relationship between *persuading consumers* and *educating minds* is the journalistic promotion of oat bran, a product which—I testify from personal experience—tastes suspiciously like shredded cardboard. When it comes to many oat-bran products, "You know and I know they don't taste good," says Kathryn Newton of General Mills, makers of Cheerios. The ad, by Saatchi & Saatchi Advertising, "is a way to educate consumers who . . . now want something a little more palatable." (*USA Today*, 1989)

Of this use of "educate" to mean "persuade," the anthropologist Jules Henry said, "In the jargon of advertising in America, *education* means educating the public to buy, and *inspiration* means inspired to buy." (Henry, 1963, p. 21) The point is not merely that advertisers and manufacturers use the term "educate" for their own ends, i.e., promoting consumption of an ever-growing range of goods and services—one expects such behavior from marketers. The dismaying point is that employing the term "educate" as synonymous with "persuade" now makes perfect sense in a society in which indoctrination and persuasion have come to be indistinguishable from education.

In effect, as Dewey observed many years ago, the forces promoting "miseducation" pervade our society and work against education, defined as cultivation of "intelligence," a term that Dewey often used as a synonym of "critical thought." (Dewey, 1922, p. 288; Shermis, 1961) In the language of systems analysis: Taking society as a whole, and assuming that the success of our economic system is based directly on depressing critical thought and questioning the economic assumptions, one could reasonably expect that young people would not be trained to think. Indeed, and more accurately, the teachers are training young consumers *not to think.*

THE MEDIA

Another cultural force is the process by which politicians are elected—or, in the consumerist language of American politics, "packaged and sold." Despite a century-long civics textbook tradition that has transmitted a verbal ideal of political participation involving citizens' analytical examination of political stands and issues, political reality is quite the opposite. (Barth and Shermis, 1980) Television's seconds-long "sound bites" featuring a visual image, a slogan, a reassuring voice-over narration with musical accompaniment, is precisely the opposite of reasoned analysis. Blame for other forces likewise depressing reflective thought can be laid at the doorstep of the print and electronic media.

Consider the format in which most significant news stories are presented. This format is premised on the assumption that the two-minute voice-over televised narration, or six-column-inch news story, is suitable treatment for most events, and that anything more detailed will take so much time that the readers' or viewers' attention might flag. Readers who are repelled by newspapers and television will, of course, not look at the all-important commercials. Thus, what cannot be squeezed into this abbreviated format is ignored.

But what can be so compressed is trivial, misleading and simplistic. "Headline" news and radio or TV news stories reduced to what can be expressed in a newspaper headline or a TV sound bite provide bits of disconnected information. The media, thus conceived, are inherently incapable of providing background, context, discussion of conflict or analysis. In Dewey's words, they cannot "signalize hidden facts, or facts seen in relation to one another, a picture of a situation on which men can act intelligently." (Dewey, 1922)

As a communication medium, television has much more to do with persuasion than with education. The very constraints of television are a Procrustean bed in which, no matter the significance, news items are deliberately expanded or contracted to meet the demands of a television format. Too lengthy stories are clipped and reduced; too brief items are padded with visual overlays, swelling music, and file film, that have little to do with the voice-over narration. The team of cameraperson and reporter may shoot many yards of videotape; however, what appears on the television screen is liable to be a short, dramatic, riveting statement, taken out of context, designed to fascinate, whether or not it educates.

Although television in the 1940s was envisioned as a means of education and entertainment, in the 1990s it is predominantly a means of persuasion. "To persuade" is the opposite of "to educate." The former requires that an individual be convinced and enticed to a point of view or course of action. Commercials accomplish the persuasive intent, as do most other television offerings—docudramas, mini-series, and even the family sit-coms that peddle middle-class morality as the American norm. The television producers of persuasion are indoctrinating viewers to certain cultural standards, and our school teachers are not teaching their students to distinguish between persuasion and education.

Persuasion moves on the assumption that there is a given, a point of view, a product, an outlook, or a belief system that must be accepted. Education goes forward on the assertion that individuals are capable of reaching a conclusion on their own, and that, given a balanced picture, they will reflect and be able to exercise reasoned choice. In persuasion, the "locus of control" is external; in education it is internal, within the individual. Education is premised on the assumption that individuals are to be respected because they are capable of making choices; persuasion is based upon the notion that individuals lack the capacity to think and must have this done for them by a presumably superior being. Americans tend to be critical of authoritarian societies that are drenched with propaganda, slogans, indoctrination, and covert or overt brainwashing. However, most students and teachers with whom I have discussed this issue have difficulty in describing how education in a democratic society ought to be different from the indoctrination that takes place in an authoritarian one.

SPECIAL-INTEREST GROUPS

A third cultural force that dampens reflective inquiry is the efforts of special-interest groups, most prominent of which are religious organizations, that view public schools as extensions of their own programs and theological agendas. To this end, these groups intimidate teachers, frightening them and their students away from themes that the ideologues regard as unacceptable. In my hometown, these forces have been almost completely successful in discouraging teachers from dealing with "values clarification," especially in the area of sexual beliefs and practices. The Texas textbook controversey over evolutionism *versus* creationism is as well-known a case of religious harassment of critical inquiry as one needs to cite; and in Kanawha County, West Virginia, the American War of Education and Religion even became a shooting war. Objective inquiry at school into a touchy public issue is discouraged because students may raise questions that parents and religious authorities cannot answer that touch upon particular sectarian dogmas and the difference between the official mores and actual practice. (Jenkinson, 1979; Hunt, 1975; Hunt and Metcalf, 1968; Shermis and Barth, 1981)

"Closed-area theory" is a position that was introduced in the early 1940s by an influential Ohio State University educator, Alan Griffin, and was picked up by his students and students of his students. (Farley, 1978; Hunt and Metcalf, 1968; Hunt, 1975; Shermis and Barth, 1983) "Closed-area theory" means that many beliefs in [our culture] are held with such emotional fervor that people holding them do not want them to be examined on a reflective, that is, critically objective or scientific, level. These ideologies are held as sacred and untouchable; critical examination is taboo. (Hunt, 1975, p. 47)

"Closed-area" theorists have concluded that even though the cultivation of critical thought has been an important part of certain reformist agendas, other forces within and without education have thus far successfully prevented schools from engaging in the freedom of the intellect that seems to be mandated by democratic theory. Whether these forces will persist into the future depends less upon the efforts of reformers and educational critics than upon the willingness of teachers to learn, and administrators to defend, the theory and practice of reflective thinking and teaching. That there are many other factors involved in this reformation is easily granted; however, if our society has learned anything about educational reform in this century, it is, first, that reform cannot be decreed from above, and second, that teachers cannot superimpose critical thinking strategies on a foundation of unexamined and incompatible teaching theory.

A Theory of Reflective Inquiry

We Begin with Dewey

Assuming that readers of this monograph wish to promote reflective thinking in their classes—at whatever grades in whatever subject—how should they proceed? First, I summarize John Dewey's conception of reflective thinking; then I discuss some of the most important elements of reflective inquiry; finally, I sketch a succinct design that one might model to implement reflective inquiry in the classroom.

In his *How We Think*, Dewey attempted to provide an alternative to rote-memory, and lockstep learning, and in so doing he elaborated upon a definition of "reflective thought." His oft-quoted definition is as follows: "Active, persistent and careful consideration of any belief or supposed form of knowledge in light of the grounds that support it and the further conclusion to which it tends." (Dewey, 1910 and 1933) (Dewey's later thoughts on the same set of themes can be found in *Logic: The Theory of Inquiry* and *Essays in Experimental Logic*, which are couched in terms more compatible to philosophers than to teachers.)

The essential meaning of Dewey's definition points in two directions. The definition proceeds from sources, origins, and justifications. It asks, What support is there for any given proposition? Does this support derive from experience, authority, logic, or intuition?

The definition then proceeds to consequences, implications, results, and ends. It asks: "Taken seriously, where would this proposal lead? What does this proposal mean in action?"

The phrase "belief or supposed form of knowledge" conveys Dewey's conviction that knowledge is of human invention and is, therefore, not to be taken as absolute, finished, or final but rather as tentative, as a *candidate* for truth. The phrase "active, persistent, and careful consideration" means that knowledge derives from a thinking process that is active, not passive; persistent, not desultory or spasmodic; and painstaking and careful, not rushed and slovenly.

In three works written after *How We Think*, namely *Human Nature and Conduct*, *The Public and Its Problems*, and *The Quest for Certainty* (Dewey, 1922, 1927, 1929), Dewey defined the opposite of "reflective thought." One form of non-reflective thought, Dewey believed, is that which is inflexibly mired in tradition and habit. Another is responses that proceed from unreflective impulse and abrupt, "brief-lived moments of violence." (Shermis, 1961, p. 9) Dewey also analyzed the tendency of humans to search for absolutes in a world of change, tragedy, and confusion in their desperate need for a "safe and secure harbor." (Dewey, 1929) Dewey kept making one point throughout his very long life: Our society continues the outworn tradition of absolutizing ideas, flattening out distinctions on opposite ends of a continuum, and refusing to think about problems in an inventive and fresh manner. This summarizes Dewey's argument about why schools have proven so resistant to encouraging reflective thought where and when it is most needed.

By no means are all proponents of reflective inquiry in agreement about every aspect of the undertaking. One unresolved problem is this: Ought one to teach critical thinking independent of a given subject matter? (deBono, 1983) A second issue is this: Is critical thought, as Dewey said it is, different from all other types of thinking? Or, as Nielsen said, is *all* thinking critical thinking? (Neilsen, 1989) The enormity of the topic, and the differences among theoreticians notwithstanding, consensus prevails on the most important points.

At the most basic level, theoreticians agree that reflective inquiry is mandated by our socio-political structure. Democracy allows considerable personal freedom, requires the consent of the governed, and tends to exist in a technologically advanced society. Such a society differs fundamentally from preliterate or traditional societies in which intellectual commonplaces are grounded in authority, and custom is a serviceable means of guidance. In a society like that, reflective thought is deemed to be unnecessary and would prove to be subversive. In democratic, technologically-driven, rapidly-changing societies, custom, authority, and tradition are likely to suffer eclipse in the face of changing cultural patterns and emerging technology. In forward-tending societies, the young will inherit a society different from the one that was handed down to their parents.

To what end should the young be educated? How much education does "everyone" need? There is an answer to both of these questions. To the question, What end or purpose does education serve, the answer has been: Education to critical inquiry in a rapidly changing, technocratic, and democratic society is for the purpose of allowing individuals to become as autonomous as they can become in an inherently ambiguous and confusing society. How much education do the citizens of such a society need? As much as they can get!

WHAT MUST ONE KNOW BEFORE THE PROCESS OF INQUIRY BEGINS?

Writers on the subject of reflective inquiry tend to agree about the relationship between reflective inquiry and the knowledge base: Reflective thinking is *not* what students do *after* they finish the lesson, *not* a different order of intellectual activity that is permitted only after the students have acquired specific content. Rather, reflective thinking is what students do in order to acquire content. Content is not a body of discrete information having no perceived connection with a learner's purpose, nor is content confined to the facts, concepts, generalizations, etc., to be found in a textbook. Content, rather, is the information needed so that someone may reflect on an important question, issue, or problem. Content must be ever expanding to include the data of reflection and the evidence from any source that bears on the problem.

Although there is no agreement on the nature, shape, and implication of any given problem, there is general accord about three assumptions: identification, internalization, and transmission. First, problem identification is the heart of the process of reflective inquiry. A set of information, implications, and causes for action needs to be identified as a problem on which critical thought can chew. Second, unless students internalize the problem by sensing it as in some way their own, there is no reason for the rest of the process that necessarily follows. Third, although teachers may very well communicate some information to their students, critical inquiry is not primarily transmission of facts, opinions, conclusions, or plans for action.

Chief among the habits of teaching as transmission that a teacher must revise is the notion that problem-solving is what students do, but that the teacher is exempt from the process. The core of the critical-inquiry teaching process is the reconstruction of experience, the totality of the problem identified for internalization and all-out problem-solving. Experience provides the source of ideas; and as one lives through and refines the process of experiencing, experience also supplies the means of reconstruction, change, and adaptation. The implication of this entire process of analysis is that teachers must *necessarily* pay attention to the students' world of experience.

THOUGHT AND EMOTION

Perhaps the piece within this complex proposition that is most difficult for administrators and teachers to embrace is that the problem must be perceived, sensed, and internalized by students. This means that before students can think reflectively, they must experience some degree of confusion, puzzlement, bewilderment, or disorientation. These, obviously, are sticky and bothersome *emotions*, and teachers tend to be intimidated by the prospect of a classroom of students expressing themselves vehemently, disagreeing with one another, and ultimately refusing to accept the teacher-approved and authoritative version of truth. In a society in which expression of emotion is considered to be not good manners, teachers, and at times students, faced with fervent beliefs, are left uneasy. Teachers also feel—with considerably more justification—that emotional expressions without a knowledge base is pointless. Students do require a knowledge base; to suppose that they might proceed without information flies in the face of *any* theory of decision-making or problem-solving. But to agree to the need for information is not to endorse the essentially elitist, rationalist notion that students must *first* acquire a knowledge base, so that only *afterwards* can they think. Critical inquiry and acquisition of information occur simultaneously, just as emotion flows immediately from thought.

Students and teacher alike, moreover, must be developing an expanding knowledge base. Conventional lists of concepts, facts, formulae, and textbook information as preconditions to thought have nothing to do with a *reflective* knowledge base. Teachers of all subjects who require students to answer after-the-chapter textbook questions and to define technical terms before they so much as ask the first question about the topic are not only not encouraging reflection but also they are breeding the tedium that accompanies most formal classroom teaching much of the time. Teachers do not want on purpose to "turn off" students to learning; and they are unaware that drill, repetition, and systematic textbook coverage accomplish precisely this undesirable end. Nevertheless, they seem unwilling to consider other approaches to subject matter or to repose confidence in themselves as a source of problem-solving teaching.

Over many years of working with teachers, I have heard them agree in principle to the proposition that when a given content failed either to stimulate or teach, then it was necessary to try different content. Having said that, however, they would vigorously defend the content into which they found themselves and their students locked. For teachers to admit that what they are doing is, admittedly, self-defeating, and then for them to continue to do as they have always done, is a recipe for turning schools into morgues.

Another practice—quite distinct from what I have just described—that is also pointless, is asking a student how he or she *feels* about an issue or problem, and then asking the same question of another student, and so on, without teacher comment or counter-question. While rap sessions and brief and heated exchanges of unreflected feelings are not necessarily a waste of time, they are not compatible with disciplined inquiry. Rap sessions require no exercise of the rules of evidence, and they are inherently incapable of producing a careful and systematic analysis, for they ignore the requirement of objective criteria. (A most useful text to read on this subject is *Reflective Teaching: The Method of Education* by H. Gordon Hullfish and Philip Smith, 1961, which is devoted entirely to one question: What does it mean to talk about grounding beliefs in a knowledge base?)

To require that a body of information be mastered prior to inquiry is not a valid description of what ordinary people do when they think.

Louis Pasteur did not study entomology before he began to inquire into the silkworm disease that almost ruined the silk industry in France in the 1860s. When he first started making critical inquiry into the problem, Pasteur did not so much as know even that the silkworm moth went through a four-stage metamorphosis. Pasteur learned what he needed to know as he went along.

Sir Alexander Fleming not only did not know what sort of mould he was examining in the first few seconds after he identified the source of what was to become penicillin, but also he was not to discover for many months that it was *Penicillium notatum* or what it could do.

A three- or four-year-old child does not need to know that a butterfly belongs to the order *Lepidoptera* before he or she asks what that lovely and amazing object is. The turned-around notion that students first need facts before thought can take place, is a self-deluding cover-up, meant to disguise teachers' largely unconscious, but profoundly felt need to transmit (presumably as an exercise in job security) a body of traditionally conceived and canonically organized content. Stated boldly, many teachers cannot tolerate reflective inquiry because they cannot imagine not transmitting content which they themselves have learned, which other teachers transmit, and which they believe themselves to be responsible to convey to their students.

Quite the other way round, I assert that what must take place before one begins to think is not the transmission and acquisition of a specific amount or kind of facts: What is needed, rather, is that someone feel impelled by awe, need, wonder or curiosity to ask a question.

KNOWLEDGE AS A FUNCTION OF A THEORY OF REALITY

Whatever might be the objective reality "out there," what individuals make of the world around them is what constitutes the only reality with which they can deal. Reality is objective, but it is perceived, only and always, subjectively. Here, we are up against the Greeks again, and it asks a great deal of teachers—or anyone else, for that matter—to depart from 2,500 years of philosophical tradition.

Siegel and Carey have made a valid point. Their argument is that individuals "...encounter a world made meaningful through the mediation of interpretants—networks of signs." (Siegel and Carey, 1989, p. 19) This phrase refers to a philosophical assumption that we do *not* come into direct relationship with external reality and the knowledge held by other minds. What we know about both knowledge and reality is mediated, understood, by means of our own languages, symbols, and signs. Individuals construct their own meaning as they interpret their objects of perception.

This conclusion requires rejection of the philosophical position known as "naive realism" as applied to knowing. This is the term for the belief that meaning is known directly from the proper contact with externally existing reality. We emphasize this point here because naive realism is the philosophical position of most teachers, whether they are aware of it or not.

What, then, is the appropriate assumption about both meaning and knowledge? The most basic philosophical conclusion is that knowledge cannot be taken as absolute. This is not the same conclusion as the assertion that knowledge does not exist or that if it did, it could not be known. (Both statements entrap the thinker in a philosophical self-contradiction; and both are absolutes.) Philosophically speaking, absolutes refer to knowledge about a reality that exists whether it is perceived or not. An absolute depends not at all upon time, place, point of view, or perception. Absolutes, like Plato's ideal forms, exist whether or not they are known. From Plato's viewpoint, one must come into the proper relationship with knowledge by apprehending the absolute. Accordingly, over the last 2,500 years, most absolutist philosophers have maintained that the teacher's function is to acquaint students with knowledge that exists externally, independent of the thinkers or their perceptions.

From the standpoint of critical inquiry, one need not bother to assert that *there are no absolutes,* but, rather, that the knowledge that we humans possess is knowledge constituted by, found in, or—to use Dewey's phrase—*wrought from human experience.* Knowledge, thus, is dynamic, not static.

Charles S. Peirce, who realized that knowledge is forever shifting, contributed the following, useful mixture of metaphors to prod our reflection:

> *[W]e never have firm rock beneath our feet; we are walking on a bog, and we can be certain only that the bog is sufficiently firm to carry us for the time being. Not only is this all the certainty that we can achieve, it is also all the certainty we can rationally wish for, since it is precisely the tenuousness of the ground that constantly prods us forward....Only doubt and uncertainty can provide a motive for seeking new knowledge.* (quoted in Siegel and Carey, 1989, p. 21)

In Peirce's and in Dewey's analyses, *all knowledge* is infused with doubt. More importantly, doubt also propels individuals to *seek* knowledge. As Dewey—who had studied under Peirce in the early 1880s at Johns Hopkins University (Boydston, 1970, p. 331)—argued, knowledge derives from a process that begins with doubt, with the need to clarify that which had been decided and settled. This is the connection between the concept "knowledge base" and "problem-solving."

Because no precise one-to-one correspondence between true perception and external reality can be assumed, knowledge is not "fact" but "artifact." An artifact, literally a "thing made by human skill," is not given but made. (Partridge, 1983, p. 27) Knowledge, from this point of view, is, likewise, not given, not dogma to be accepted as self-evidently true, but individually and socially constructed. Any particular item of knowledge is not something that has been verified and established firmly and is therefore "objective," or, in student dialect, a "true fact." Neither is knowledge reducible to a large body of "true facts," or of assertions and propositions that can or must be known on their own terms. To assume this organization of knowledge removes learners from the process by which the knowledge was constructed, and it turns them into passive spectators, the philosphical equivalent of those who collect coins instead of making money, or collect baseball cards instead of playing the game. When human beings are active—and this is the cornerstone of reflective inquiry—their role changes from passive acquisitors to active investigators.

THE SUBJECTIVE/OBJECTIVE DUALISM

Twentieth-century philosophy, informed by Einstein's theory of relativity, has avoided the absolute distinction between "objective" and "subjective." (Snygg and Combs, 1949) That which is known and is considered objective must be known by a *someone*, and that someone sees the world from what E. E. Bayles called "an angle of envisionment" (Bayles, 1960), a synonym for perspective or point of view. Bayles and Dewey are consistent with Harste's contention that "thinking critically is a matter of reading signs." The signs are not "there"; they are invented by humans to "make reflective thinking possible" (Harste, introduction, Siegel and Carey, 1989). The traditional objective/subjective dualism is in part responsible for the development of passive teaching strategies, for if humans are passive and subjective learners, and if knowledge is objectively true on-its-own-terms, then the only function of learners is to reproduce precisely what is out there. This is a model for frustrated teachers, bored students, cramming for exams, objective test items, high drop-out rates, and alienation.

KNOWLEDGE AS PLURALISTIC

Knowledge, therefore, is not like a graven image, fixed, immutable, and demanding uncritical worship. Neither is knowledge singular and monotheistic, a subject grasping the knower as object. Nor is it knowledge like Plato's representations of the One—a perfect, unchanging, single source. Knowledge is, rather, multivalent and plural in its powers and forms.

An examination of the processes by which humans contrive knowledge reveals that there are many kinds of knowledge gained in many different ways. The knowledge of chemists is not precisely the same as the knowledge of biologists, literary critics, physicians, or sculptors. Nor should it be assumed that all knowledge, to be true, must approach some ideal source of knowledge (which, in the last hundred years or so, has been thought to be physics). Different kinds of knowledge assume different ways of devising and gaining knowledge, with different kinds of verification processes.

In sum, reflective teaching is not a matter of a student coming into a relationship with a knowledge base that exists on its own terms. It is not a matter of acquainting students with a body of knowledge that exists independently of perception. Reflective thinking *is* a matter of helping students to acquire that knowledge which is essential for their thinking about a matter significant to them. Knowledge, therefore, can be methodologically defined as *the data of inquiry*. This admittedly abstract phrase means that content is whatever clues, evidence, or data one can discover in the search for a solution to a given problem.

This notion of content rests on the working assumption that the inquiry process begins with a question that must be answered or a problem that must be solved. The phrase "must be answered," moreover, means that someone *perceives* that a given problem, issue, question, or topic is important enough to require a solution. We are all familiar with what happens when students have their curiosity piqued: Hands fly up in all directions, and one question follows another, with students energetically talking and listening to one another. Teachers frequently permit this kind inquiry to persist for a little while, and then they announce that we had all better get back to the book, please, so turn to page 197. The matter that aroused the interest and concern is taken to have been a tangent. On the contrary, such occasions of spirited inquiry are—from the perspective of reflective thinking—not a mere tangent, but rather the point of it all.

I treat this issue at length because teachers tend to persuade students that if "it" is in a textbook, then "it" is true, verified, and valid. When students reach universities, they are always surprised to learn that textbook knowledge has been built by humans, that humans disagree with one another, that the knowledge found in last year's edition of a text has been supplanted by this year's edition, and that in many fields of inquiry, textbook knowledge is dated and obsolete before it is published. (Even knowledge in journal articles, perhaps only a few months old, may be obsolete.) The universal tendency of teachers, in all societies, to require only memorization and acceptance of textual knowledge is based upon lack of understanding of how knowledge is actually produced. When knowledge is regarded as changing and dynamic, of human invention, pluralistic (i.e., assuming many forms), and when knowledge as *product* is separated from knowledge as *process*, then one realizes that most classroom traditions, conventions, and practices are either inappropriate to, or inconsistent with, reflective inquiry.

The appropriate assumption to make, I suggest, is this: Construction of knowledge as a human product requires that students and teachers together share in the process of inquiry and discovery. The teacher is not above this process, and the students ought not to be left out of it; they are all necessarily a part of it. The teacher's role is not to ask the "right" question and be the ultimate source of all answers. If the question or problem that motivated the inquiry process is significant, then the answers are unlikely to be simple. Students must be encouraged to frame their own questions about the problem so that it can be pursued on a rational basis, motivated by their own will to understand and know. Extended time must be found to probe, examine, and explore.

Thoughtful Reader, you may raise an objection at this point with regard to my statement about the impermanence and fluidity of knowledge: "What about the alphabet and the multiplication tables? Neither has recently undergone any significant changes!"

To be sure. The Roman alphabet evolved out of its Indo-European, Semitic, Greek, and Latin antecedents, as knowledge gained in this century about its historical development has demonstrated. It has served our purposes very well, largely intact for two millennia. As with all other forms of knowledge, however, the alphabet, the number system, and arithmetic functions (such as the multiplication tables) are all of human coinage. Our number system is an arbitrary invention, which makes sense *only if a base 10 is assumed*. It, too, is a convention, albeit a useful and time-tried one, and it did not work nearly so well until the Arabs invented the zero.

Elementary teachers who insist only upon memorization, and who indoctrinate both the alphabet and the multiplication tables as if both were dogmas, do a disservice to their students. They make it unlikely that their students will later be able to cope with binary computer languages, or base-eight systems, non-Euclidean geometry, Einsteinian physics, or any other scientific, literary, philosophic, or artistic *inventions*. If reading and mathematics methods educators who prepare teachers for teaching in elementary schools agree upon anything, it is that children learn better when they come to understand the underlying relationships of words, letters, sounds, and syntax of the English language. By the same token, children comprehend basic arithmetic functions when they grasp the underlying logical structure of mathematics. To learn both language and arithmetic in this way is to learn knowledge as a human invention.

VALUES

Even as some philosophical assumptions about knowledge are incompatible with reflective inquiry, so also some assumptions about values and valuing are also inconsistent. The first wrong-headed assumption is that values come from another world that is unrelated and opposite to the world of knowledge. This assumption is at work in the student question that invariably is asked immediately after an assignment is made: "Do you want *just* the facts, or can we give our opinions?" The answer—"I want your opinion to be supported by facts"—is usually considered by my students to be an outright evasion. This answer, however, is premised upon philosophical assumptions different from those that students employ: Their question is based upon the assumption that an answer is *either* factual or opinion; the answer is based on the assumption, consistent with reflective inquiry, that values, opinions, attitudes, judgments, and decisions are one with facts, data, information, and knowledge.

The world of knowing ought not to be kept apart from the world of values. The reason for this is complex, depending as much upon the findings of psychologists and social scientists during the 20th century as it does on the thought of philosophers and "hard" scientists. (Bigge, 1971) However, the notion of a positive/normative distinction—i.e., "that which is" as distinct from "that which ought to be"—is a philosophical dualism from which social scientists have only recently retreated.

Dewey pointed out that the knowledge/value distinction is part of the 2,400-year legacy of Greek dualisms that has proven to be as tenacious as it is distorting. (Shermis, 1960; Bode, 1940) In the real world where people make decisions and act upon choices, what we know, or think we know, and what we perceive as preferable, are inseparable. In the real world, individuals must decide whether to go to graduate school, work, or do something else. They must choose between buying a new car or fixing the old clunker. They must choose between staying put in the job and town where they have lived for many years and where their children are quite happy, or starting over in a new, challenging, better-paying position. Finally, as teachers, they must figure out whether to grade homework papers, of which they are heartily sick but which, they announced, would be returned tomorrow morning, or whether they should take the evening off to relax. All such value decisions are reached with respect to "facts." Or, to put it more accurately, decisions are made in the context of experience that always includes "oughts" and "shoulds" as well as the "truths" and "realities" that we habitually call facts.

The notion that white-coated scientists operate in a value vacuum, pursuing "hard" facts which exist regardless of who sees them, is another part of the distorting legacy of Greek dualisms. From the standpoint of 20th-century epistemology, scientists perform research within a *frame of reference*. They see the world through lenses composed of familiar concepts, cultural values, expectations conditioned by years of experience, and theories that follow some *preferred* set of norms. A scientific frame of reference, in short, is an organizing pattern in which the world of objectivity and perception are inseparable from subjectivity and conception. If this were not the case, how else can one explain why, using the *same* skeletal remains, physical anthropologists cannot agree whether the famous owner of the well-known skeleton called "Lucy" spent most of her life walking on all fours or whether she stood upright, ambling along with a bipedal gait. (*Science News*, 1971; Johanson and Shreeve, 1989) If this were not the case, why is it that astronomers with the *same* data on the center of our galaxy cannot decide whether the Milky Way is inhabited by a black hole or something else equally bizarre?

According to the traditional argument, the "correspondence theory of truths," galaxies and prehistoric hominids are whatever they are, regardless of what people know or believe. Hence, as soon as people have collected enough "facts," they will agree and gain true knowledge of human evolution and black holes. This argument is difficult to rebut convincingly, for it has become part of the way we in the Western World have learned to perceive and believe. Nevertheless, many scientists and philosophers of science in the 20th century gradually abandoned naive realism and a theory of neutral conformity to external reality. While there may be a reality out there, independent of any perceiver, what any given individual, scientist or not, says about that reality reflects how he or she has learned to think about the world. No matter how precisely accurate and factual anyone's statement about external hard facts may be, there will be some subjective element in the statement. There may be an objective world that exists independently of you and me and everyone else, but the only reality that you and I or anyone else can deal with is that which comes into us by way of our sensory impressions, and then gets interpreted according to our individual sets of previous experiences, presuppositions, and the other highly subjective aspects of our personal and cultural conditioning. Reality is what we make of what comes into us, what we interpret of what we perceive the world to be.

TRANSMISSION AS THE RESULT OF A PHILOSOPHICAL POSITION

Many commentators have bemoaned the reduction of teaching to transmission, but the continuing persistence of the habit suggests that it must be deeply embedded in Western society, going back to the time before books when teaching consisted largely of passing on the oral tradition. But teaching as transmission is more than mere cultural bias; the practice logically flows from certain philosophical conceptions. These philosophical conceptions are so widespread that they form an invisible part of the social environment. Because these assumptions are invisible, they go un-identified and hence can work their mischief endlessly. Transmission, i.e., the simple conveying of information from the mouths or pages of an authority to the pens and ears of students, is consistent with assumptions descending from an authoritarian past. But transmission, I am arguing, is simply inconsistent with the aims of critical thinking and teaching in a political democracy. In an authoritarian society, or one governed by an official ideology such as Marxian ideology in the USSR or the ideology of Qaddafi in Libya, truths are official truths and they must be accepted, certain questions must not be asked, and certain topics are off limits. Deviation from orthodoxy is a very serious transgression, and it may be severely punished.

Although curriculum is taken to be objective and canonical, in fact, someone has made a selection that was based on their own subjective perceptions. All curriculum makers, like all historians, pick and choose what they wish to include in textbooks. Over the years, the tradition in U. S. history has been to emphasize political, diplomatic, and military history, and either to scant or ignore intellectual, social, and industrial history. This norm of selection reflects a largely unconscious cultural preference, but teachers and students, unaware of these biases, are convinced that what is in textbooks is both adequate, objective, and largely factual. That is, texts consist of "facts" which are taken to be synonymous with "knowledge" that is inherently worthy of acquiring. While it certainly is the case that students need facts—knowledge, information, and data with which to think—it is not the case that teaching must be reduced to transmitting concepts mislabeled "knowledge" or "fact."

One way of grasping that traditional transmission is self-defeating in its obfuscation of "fact" and "knowledge" is by reading the following citation from a volume in my large collection of antique textbooks. These especially vicious lines come from a manual used by county superintendents to examine teachers and students in the Midwest in the 19th century. This text demonstrates the degree to which a society transmits its culturally derived, socially constructed civic values to students through textbooks and schools.

> *Question:* Give a brief description of the American Indians as they have manifested themselves to the Whites....

> *Answer:* The Indians are cruel, treacherous, revengeful; and although boastful of their willingness for war, have ever shown themselves, as a race, cowardly in open battle. They are lazy and improvident,—the lessons of famine teaching them nothing for the future. The women are degraded, and regarded by the men as only fit to bear the burdens of their lords and provide for their daily wants. (Brown, pp. 175, 195)

This extraordinary bit of bigotry—in which Indians are described as both warlike and cowardly—is but one of a large number of possible illustrations to demonstrate that "traditional" does not signify "valid." A century ago, this teaching of contempt toward other human beings was a painful expression of bad memories left over from the Indian Wars, wars which the European invaders themselves had started. Swallowing hard, one may think of this point of view as "the conventional wisdom of the time" transmitted and received by Anglo-European heirs of Indian fighters as simple "fact" and reliable "knowledge." Now, upon critical reflection, one would perceive this bit of transmitted wisdom to have been nothing more than a social construct then, bigotry now, and too culturally subjective ever to have passed the test of being factually informed knowledge.

Although traditional teaching may appear to be blessed by time and familiarity, most tradition does not provide an adequate basis for making decisions, acquiring knowledge, or adopting values. To say that "good boys and girls" are polite and respectful because that is the way our social tradition defines acceptable children, is to ignore the same tradition which also says that "good boys and girls" are honest, forthright, and candid. Anyone who believes that it is possible for a given child to be both respectful and polite *and also* forthright and candid, has not raised children—or at least has not reflected on the hundreds of little decisions in which these two sets of values are not compatible. Our tradition sanctifies a large number of values, many of which are mutually incompatible, inconsistent, and contradictory.

Were reflective inquiry to be introduced into schools tomorrow, however, fact-gathering would work a different way. Students would require considerably more facts than they either now have at their disposal or can take notes on from a teacher's transmission lecture during one of those all-too-short academic hours. Students would be encouraged to seek as much data as they could find, from whatever source they could find it. Teachers would not hear, "Will this be asked on the exam?"— that blood-chilling question that betrays the assumption that the only knowledge worth pursuing is that which reappears as exam fodder. Further, the practice of using a *single* textbook, the contents of which are memorized and passively received rather than examined and actively criticized, would immediately vanish. Texts, especially for use in grades 1–12, are typically arranged encyclopedically, but encyclopedias are not designed to be read systematically, from beginning to end, or with particular enjoyment. They are used as a resource for data-collection when one needs certain kinds of information. This is precisely the judicious use that teachers should encourage their students to make of textbooks. Don't read it like a Bible, but rather, pick and choose and compare and question.

DISCUSSION AS THE HEART OF INQUIRY

The heart of reflective inquiry is not texts or lectures but discussion. Teachers of all subjects no longer need to spend their time transmitting "basic information," a practice which prevailed when books were few and precious, crafted painstakingly by calligraphers and illuminators, and then chained to library tables. In the Middle Ages, teachers had little function but to transmit through lectures the knowledge found in a relatively few classical or religious sources. Afterwards they would ask questions designed to see whether their students had memorized the sacred tradition. (The exceptions to these purveyors of transmission are a relatively few creative few, e.g., Peter Abelard, the Latin Averroists, Thomas Aquinas, whose fame as arousers and stimulators of the European community of scholars spread throughout their own times and into ours.) The invention of movable type, which transformed the world *outside* of schools and universities after the 1450s, has not had sufficient impact on teaching. (McCluhan, 1980) Similarly, the proliferation of electronic devices in the second half of the 20th century, which has vastly multiplied the amount of information available, has not noticeably affected what teachers do in classrooms.

Most critics of education in America have argued that the world needs individuals who can assess, appraise, and interpret information, and solve problems of unprecedented magnitude. To teach students these high-level thinking skills requires a radically different orientation to knowledge, facts, values, teaching, and testing. This orientation would depart fundamentally from pre-Gutenberg practices based on the assumption that students must receive information *now* which they will then store for use *later*.

WHAT IS A REFLECTIVE DISCUSSION?

A reflective inquiry discussion is not the equivalent of a *recitation*. Recitations usually involve rehashing of concepts that students were supposed to "understand," wherein the teacher plays the more prominent role, largely explanatory and expository. In a reflective discussion, to the contrary, the teacher asks students to raise questions, to cite evidence, and to respond to queries about the meaning and validity of their knowledge:

❖ How do you know this?

❖ Does everyone understand this in the same way?

❖ What is the source of your understanding?

❖ How accurate, valid, contemporary, comprehensive or understandable is this?

❖ Is what you have just said (cited, referred to) a fact? That is, was it derived empirically by observing something that *happened* in time and space?

❖ If not a fact, is it a concept?

❖ Is it part of a theory? Is it a cultural prejudice, custom, or convention?

For instance, is the assertion a *fact* that Israel, Iraq, and Egypt are in the Middle East?

What seems like a simple enough question of geography is, however, full of traps.

The term "Middle East" was coined when England was the center of the world, and these countries were to the east of Greenwich, farther east than Turkey, but not so far as China, which was in the Far East. "Middle East" is a linguistic convention based upon a 19th-century Eurocentric view of the world—just as much of what we tend to think of as given and permanent is also Eurocentric.

For another instance, is it a *fact* that a wristwatch is a timepiece worn around the wrist with a band? No. This is a definition of a specific object, not an observable *fact*. Is it a fact that 2 + 2 = 4? No. This is a logical process, not an empirical happening. Is it a *fact* that Lincoln was our greatest president? No. This is a disputable value judgment, albeit one held widely by both the public and American historians, though not by many Southerners. Is it a *fact* that boys do not *ever* slug girls? I'll let *you* answer that! Is it a *fact* that gentlemen never slug ladies? That, of course, depends on your definition of "ladies" and "gentlemen," but it cannot be a *fact*. Statements about who gets to swat whom are tied in with the culture, contrary to the wishes of those who suppose there are universal moral standards.

Reader, if you begin to feel apprehensive because you sense your knowledge to be inadequate, so much the better! In a reflective discussion, not only must teachers possess knowledge in their field but also they must be sophisticated about the acquisition, verification, and meaning of knowledge *in philosophical terms*. This philosophical sophistication, however, needs to be translated—largely into a questioning strategy.

❖ Is what you have said accurate?

❖ Did you phrase it precisely, or is every other phrase "you know," "and that stuff," "sorta," "like," and other brainless locutions?

❖ Is it complete?

❖ Is it relevant?

❖ Does this critical term mean what you want it to mean?

❖ What do *you* think it means?

❖ What do others think it means?

❖ What support do you have for your utterance?

❖ What *kind* of support is it?

❖ Is it founded in logic?

❖ Does it have an empirical context?

❖ Is it a value judgment, or does it derive from another value judgment, and if so, what is this judgment?

❖ Is it your own judgment? If you didn't invent it, who did?

- ❖ For what purpose?

- ❖ Could it be that what you have called a "fact" is a definition or belongs to one of the other categories of discourse mentioned above?

Students usually dislike being told that what they had always taken to be a fact, a given, a truth, is nothing of the sort. A case in point is discussion of the term "egalitarian" in a sociology class, "equity" in an education class, "equal rights" in a philosophy class, the phrase "all men are created equal" in a political-science class, the maxim "in God's eyes, all souls are created equal" in a religion class, or "B + 2(x-1) = 23 in a math class. In none of these phrases does "equal" refer to a *fact*. In all of these phrases, "equal" means something different.

The widely quoted and wrongly attributed phrase about all men being created equal is an example of misunderstanding within our culture that is almost universal and complete. Not only does the Constitution *not* talk about "a self-evident truth that all men are created equal," but when Jefferson *et al.* employed this term in the Declaration of Independence, they did so to validate a social revolution. Indeed, if anything was a "self-evident truth" at those slave-owning times and in rigidly caste-ridden Europe, it was that all men came into life *unequal*.

The questioning strategy rolls on:

- ❖ Does support given an assertion descend from an authority?

- ❖ If so, which authority?

After all, Karl Marx, the King James Bible, *The Thoughts of Mao Tse Tung*, and *Webster's Third International Dictionary* are all authorities. However, some of these authorities are not recognized as such by many, and some are mutually exclusive. All of them require some degree of expertise to employ intelligently. Since most of us are lamentably short of expertise in most areas, authorities ultimately depend on our faith for their acceptance. What is the relevance or value of this discussion of authority and authority figures? Students cannot become critical thinkers unless they are able to evaluate any knowledge claim, most especially those resting upon an authority. Because most students have been trained to repose uncritical faith in one or more authorities, this is a tall order; nevertheless, in the words of a once widely-worn button and bumper sticker, we much teach our critically thoughtful students to "Question Authority."

If discussion is the heart of inquiry teaching, then probing questions are the heart of discussion. A probing question is the one that is asked in order to find out more about a question that has already been raised. The purpose of a probing question is to get students to provide more information, more clarification, and more explanation. The purpose of asking probing questions is to make it possible for teachers and students to evaluate each other's thinking.

The uses of questioning strategy are many:

- ❖ providing or eliciting simple information
- ❖ asking for clarification of a concept
- ❖ bouncing one student's idea off another
- ❖ requesting explanations
- ❖ requesting definitions
- ❖ asking for the sources of information
- ❖ evaluating those sources
- ❖ seeking examples and illustrations
- ❖ seeing how students respond to exceptions to generalizations, and to information that is deliberately discordant—a technique designed to test meaning

The typical instructional questioning strategy is appallingly deficient. Many teachers are content to ask Bloom I, low-level, factual, or memory-level questions, and wait for a brief answer; then they lecture briefly off the top of the student's answer. Not only is this an excruciatingly boring approach but also it does not help students to learn or think. A steady diet of low-level or recall questions depresses reflective inquiry.

My experience suggests, nevertheless, that asking upper-level questions *only* is of and by itself not sufficient. What is necessary is that a teacher possess a *questioning strategy*, which is an organized, flexible set of discussion questions having a wide variety of functions. (Hunkins, 1972) A teacher's questioning strategy ought not to become fixed at any one level but must be tailored to the task at hand. Alternating high- with low-level questions; asking probing questions; asking students to defend, support, explain, illustrate, and expand—all are at the heart of reflective inquiry.

Nor is it the case that *only* teachers may ask probing questions in classrooms. In a vigorous, give-and-take classroom, students need to feel free to ask one another and the teacher questions of all kinds—probing questions, refutations, requests for clarification, and support for any idea, no matter how unpopular, idiosyncratic, or—in student talk—"weird."

Internalizing Problems

Problem-Solving and Reflective Inquiry

Reflective thought begins only when a problem is perceived. If there is no problem to occasion reflective thought, if there is nothing to think about, then, in Dewey's words, what follows is a pale and insubstantial simulation of thought. Thus, teachers who wish to promote reflective inquiry must first help students identify problems.

Pseudo-Problems

Fortunately, problem identification is easier than it sounds, Granted, teachers experience great difficulty in helping students identify fruitful problems, and one problem, which a colleague and I have labeled "semantic" (Barth and Shermis, 1978), tends to defeat teachers. Defeat can be turned to a win-win classroom situation when one makes a clear distinction between a "problem exercise" and an "inquiry problem." Problem exercises abound in textbooks, workbooks, classroom discussions, and most learning situations. A problem exercise is a simple question or exercise designed to teach students a particular conclusion or skill or to impart a specific attitude.

Think of the old "word problem" algebraic saw: "If Train A leaves a station going 90 miles an hour headed north, and Train B leaves the same station, headed in the same direction, one hour later but traveling at 110 miles an hour, when will train B catch up with Train A?" The purpose of this question is to teach beginning algebra students to conceptualize a problem in such a way that the words are converted into a mathematical procedure. As such, this exercise is mildly useful; calling it a "problem," however, introduces confusion. When I, as a high-school student during an undistinguished career in Algebra One, was faced with the Train A / Train B problem, I never really *cared* if Train B *ever* caught up with Train A. It simply was not *my problem*.

PROBLEMS MUST BE FELT

For a problem to be an inquiry problem, students must feel a sense of tension. Problems compel a person to explain a situation perceived as confusing. Problems demand that individuals clear away whatever has disturbed a previously settled state of affairs. Without the disturbance, there is no internalized problem. Unless someone actually feels tension, concern, interest, inquisitiveness, and curiosity, there is no problem. Without a problem, there is no reflective thought. To ask teachers and students to tolerate ambiguity and discomfort temporarily for the sake of long-term benefits to be gained, is not a request to be made lightly, but without this cognitive ambivalence, ambiguity, and discomfort, there is no problem.

Teachers sometimes have difficulties in finding appropriate problems—those which students can feel, and which, if explored, lead to interesting, fruitful, informed learning. I have no simple formula for finding riveting questions, but here are some guidelines:

HOW DO TEACHERS KNOW THAT A PROBLEM EXISTS?

It often happens in a classroom that something "catches fire," students' behaviors undergo changes, and the classroom atmosphere becomes more emotionally charged. This is because fruitful topics and questions are usually accompanied by changes in posture, facial expressions, and other non-verbal behaviors. Students tend to sit up straighter, listen more carefully, volunteer observations, ask questions, become animated in their discourse, and show other signs inadequately described when we say that something is "interesting."

CULTIVATING PROBLEMS

When a teacher becomes aware that a problem has arisen (where the problem originated is unimportant) then there are some next steps that need to be taken. The teacher needs to realize that a particular student who raises a question, for example, about whether one can get AIDS from casual contact, is asking a question that has been raised by millions of others and which reflects widespread confusion and fear about the manner in which the disease is transmitted. The question raised by one student often does not reflect merely personal or private concerns. Indeed, the distinction between a "social" problem and a "personal" problem is arbitrary and unhelpful. (Metcalf *et al.,* 1966) All personal problems stem from the larger social context, and they are reflected in the lives, thinking, and questions of individuals. Put another way, all individual problems exist because there are social problems. It is not the case that this *one* individual is unemployed, substance-addicted, or a victim of racial prejudice. Individual problems have their roots in a larger social problem; problems called "unemployment," "drug abuse," and "bigotry" are social problems *and* individual problems. (Shermis and Barth, 1983)

Classroom discussion taking place in an effective reflective inquiry classroom follows certain rules of play:

1. Any inquiry question requires information that cannot be limited to one source or to one intellectual discipline. Questions and problems allow data from any source, whether the source is defined as a part of the formal discipline of the course, or not. Data originating from radio, TV, newspapers, magazines, friends, and relatives—all presumptive knowledge that students volunteer is admissible. A statement that begins with "My father says...." cannot simply go unacknowledged, even though teachers find information derived from a parent or other relative to be the most intimidating. It would be suicidal for a teacher to reply, "Your father is a dunce and doubtless has little reliable information on this topic." A better response: "That is what your father says; I am wondering what *you* think." If the student, not surprisingly, agrees with his

father, the next question is, "Why, then, do you agree with him?"

2. Reflective-inquiry classrooms constitute a truly egalitarian setting: All statements from any source are equally suspect. Anyone may ask any question about any supposed datum from any source because ground rules for students apply equally to teachers. The teacher has no privileged position and any rules of procedure binding students also bind teachers. Any other assumption is likely to generate an authoritarian classroom and its accompaniment, indoctrination, cynicism, and deepened rejection of adults and adult authority.

3. Teachers and students alike need to recognize that a great deal of supposed information is pick-up knowledge, information that students apparently plagiarize from dust in the air. This alleged knowledge, like a pick-up date in a sleazy bar, is typically not examined for accuracy, completeness, consistency, meaning, and other cognitive diseases, but such information is the stock-in-trade of most students—and of everyone else at one time or another. Pick-up knowledge may be used as data in a discussion, but, like any other type of evidence, even that deriving from more respectable sources, even that flowing from the mouths of teachers, it must be open to examination.

4. It is virtually certain that issues and questions raised in a reflective-inquiry class will carry students into areas replete with controversy. This is to be expected, and, indeed, it is unavoidable. With tact, respect for students' feelings and sensibilities, and concern for fairness, *any* topic—no matter how controversial, touchy, or debatable—can be intelligently and safely treated. Reflective inquiry necessarily involves the unknown, incomplete, confusing, sensitive, and controversial. Adults are notorious for keeping some subjects "off limits" to youngsters, so, naturally, questions that arise out of these closed areas are precisely the ones which fascinate students the most. Teachers who refuse to allow students to inquire into a closed area are paradoxically rejecting precisely that which engenders motivation to learn.

Granted, most of the teachers whom I have taught feared that opening up to any topic whatsoever would result in their being targeted by some community member who rejected academic freedom. My response to the fearful is to shift the burden from ourselves as individual teachers to the profession as a whole: Opposition to freedom of inquiry is not *your* problem and *my* problem and *our* problem alone; it is the concern of the entire disorganized teacher workforce. Without academic freedom and autonomy, there is no hope of promoting reflective thinking. Without the freedom to study, read, and discuss any valid topic—an opportunity that exists by-and-large at major research institutions, but, I admit, not in many public schools—reflective thinking and teaching are inconceivable.

PROBLEMS DIRECT INQUIRY

Dewey pointed out that the way a problem is phrased shapes the subsequent course of investigation. Put another way, the way the problem is sensed and conceptualized largely shapes and configures the solution.

For instance, defining the "problem of drug addiction" as too-easy access to drugs from South America, is likely to suggest a specific "solution," e.g. a "war-on-drugs" attempt to prevent the entry of drugs at the border or from the sea. To define the "problem of drug addiction" as stemming from intolerable pressures on the young, is likely to dictate some mixture of education and counseling. To define the "problem of drug addiction" as "caused" by physicians overprescribing drugs because they are miseducated by market-minded pharmaceutical houses, would probably lead to consideration of steps requiring greater federal control of this industry. To define "the problem of drug addiction" as a structural fault in which society tells individuals that the cure for any problem—personal, interpersonal, physical, psychological—comes out of a bottle, is to steer the course of investigation into cultural patterns, especially conflicting patterns of values.

In a sense, there are no problems "out there" that must be defined in a certain, prescribed manner. There are external conditions that may be defined in various ways, but how they are cast into problematic terms for the sake of reflective inquiry is completely open. Anyone may define a problem however he or she sees fit, but the definer is obliged to defend the definitional process.

A MODEL OF REFLECTIVE TEACHING IN ACTION

In some classrooms, reflective teaching and thinking does take place. When this happens, students—even so-called "reluctant learners"—participate more actively, listen better, communicate better, and learn more.

Question: What happens specifically in a reflective teaching situation that does not occur in ordinary classrooms?

Answer: The indispensably important characteristic is that reflective teaching always begins with a problem, *one that is felt and identified as such by the students.*

Question: What are the behavioral indications that students have actually identified a problem?

Answer: When students "own" a problem, they do some or all of the following:

❖ wave their hands and are eager to contribute

❖ express feelings about the matter

❖ tend to disagree with one another

❖ tend to disagree with themselves: Their answers contain self-contradictions; they are ambivalent because they are in a state of cognitive conflict, and are engaged in doing more than merely satisfying the teacher.

❖ utter statements that are uninformed and lack support

❖ substitute fear and wishful thinking for rational expression

❖ manifest signs of curiosity

- ❖ put forth a mixture of the following:
  - information and misinformation
  - inconsistency and self-contradiction
  - fears and anxieties
  - ignorance, distortions, and "factoids" (my term to denote things that sound like facts but are not)

These characteristics are present in all students in a reflective-learning situation, whether at the kindergarten, middle-school, high-school, university, or graduate-school level. Consider the following hypothetical situations:

JACK AND THE BEANSTALK

The kindergarten or first-grade teacher is reading the canonical fairy tale, *Jack and the Beanstalk*. When she has determined that students have been able to identify the main characters and, in particular, our hero, Jack; and the villain, the giant; and can summarize the plot, she then might engage in a question-and-answer session like this, starting with a seemingly innocent question:

Q: "What did Jack do when he got to the giant's castle?"

A: Jack hid from the giant, found the goose that lays golden eggs, was discovered by the giant, fled, reached the bottom of the vine, and then chopped it down. The giant, of course, tumbles down, breaks his neck, and Jack lives happily ever after with his mother and his newly found wealth.

Q: "Did Jack trespass illegally?" (In kindergarten terms, "Did Jack go into someone's house where he did not belong?")

A: "Yes!"

Q: "Did Jack steal the goose the lays golden eggs?"

A: "Yes!"

Q: "Did Jack, then, refuse to give back what did not belong to him?"

A: "Yes!"

Q: "Then did Jack escape down the bean vine and cause the giant to be killed?"

A: "Yes!"

Q: "If Jack trespassed, stole, and murdered the giant, why is the giant the villain of this story?"

The purpose of this question is not simply to fix the plot line, characters, setting, etc., in the minds of children, although this will probably happen. The purpose is to raise a challenge to the traditional and assumed conclusion that Jack is the hero, and the giant the villain. This reversed, upside-down way of perceiving culturally transmitted wisdom is designed to introduce a problem. It raises questions about the nature of heroism, morality, paradoxes, and the meaning of choice.

THE CLAIMS OF FRIENDSHIP AND OF HONESTY

Elementary school teachers have been charged with teaching good character and developing right moral convictions. This usually consists of 1) verbalizing the right words, 2) using whatever is available to drive home the message, e.g., literature, such as allegories, fairy stories, and "children's literature"; national heroes such as George Washington; and holidays, such as Thanksgiving, and 3) becoming a role model for students. No teachers would deny that this is what they do. However, many teachers are unaware that, given the history of value conflict and confusion in our society, "good values" often conflict with one another. Thus, teachers and students can begin with a general discussion of, for example, what friendship means, how friends behave toward one another, and why it is important to be a good friend. Then the teacher presents a situation:

"Assume that you are taking a test, and your best friend, who is sitting next to you, whispers, 'Move your elbow!'"

Here, an effective teacher pauses; then, poses the question: "Should you move your elbow?"

Whichever answer a student gives will raise questions from the others about the meaning of morality in the real world. If a student says that he or she would move the elbow for the express purpose of allowing the friend to copy the answer, the student is manifestly guilty of aiding and abetting cheating. Because cheating is a form of dishonesty, which is said to be immoral, the student is clearly siding with corrupt behavior. If, on the other hand, the student states that he or she would refuse to move the elbow, then clearly a friend is not being helpful. If being helpful and supportive have been upheld as important characteristics of friendship in earlier discussion—which is very likely—then the student is guilty of not being a good friend.

Does this example strike you, Reader, as likely to develop a conflict state? But, that is precisely the point and the desired pedagogical goal: Moral conflict exists in the real world; teachers ought to use this conflict instructively and not exclude it from the classroom. Further, in the hands of skilled and understanding teachers, students can deal with a complex question such as this one: "What *does* one do when the value of honesty conflicts with the demands of friendship?"

Some students may hit upon an interesting synthesis: The one who refuses to move the elbow is not thereby being a bad friend; a friend does not help a friend to cheat and swindle other friends for the dubious purpose of gaining a slight advantage in a test. Other students may reason in the other direction: What does it matter whether one does well or poorly on a given test, anyway? Maybe there are extentuating reasons for which a friend needs a little "extra help." A friend does not judge another friend's motives. Students may also begin to evaluate teaching procedures in which competition and winning are so important that people will do anything to pass tests and come out ahead. (For an absorbing account of the extent to which athletic competition has compromised and corrupted universities, see "Reforming College Sports: How? When? Ever?" *Academe*, January-February, 1991.)

Other students may answer, "I know what I *should* do, but I also know what I probably *would* do." This reply is the perfect indicator that young people learn the right words for morality but that these words may have little relationship with behavior in a crunch. Such is the divided human heart, and that is what I mean by "problems" for discussion during a session of critical inquiry.

INTERDISCIPLINARY PROBLEMS INVOLVING SCIENCE

From the earliest years of the 20th century, many national committee reports concluded that few can understand social problems without some awareness of the scientific components necessarily involved in all social problems. Thus, questions involving the use of pesticides; the damming of rivers; the disposal of solid, chemical, and radioactive waste, all require knowledge of public policy issues. Because some degree of scientific knowledge is also required, an interdisciplinary approach to applied science is commendable. Biology classes frequently include a topic called "the food chain," how animals in successive layers predate upon each other, from the microscopic one-celled organisms on the bottom, to insects, fish, birds, mammals, and human beings at the top, until it starts over again with the worms.

Even though formal recommendations stretching over a century strongly urged that public policy issues ought to be related to scientific knowledge, this tended to happen only at the university level, and often not even there. Social-science professors are not trained in the hard sciences, and natural scientists are not usually trained in the social sciences. Teachers who have some courses in the physical, natural, and social sciences are not ordinarily provided with any coursework in which they are asked to combine data from different disciplines. Given this context, how would a public policy/scientific topic be handled?

The introductory inquiry question at a middle- or high-school level might be, "How many of you believe that over-use of pesticides is ecologically destructive?" In all likelihood, many students would answer in the affirmative since this issue has received wide coverage in popular magazines, daily newspapers, public radio and television. The next question could well be posed not to the class but to a local farmer, who if he or she could not be there in person might be interviewed on audio- or videotape. The questions to the farmer might be these: "What would happen if you were not allowed to spray pesticides on your crops? What would happen if you were forbidden by law to introduce diethylstilbesterol (a growth hormone) into your livestock feed?" The farmer would very likely state that farm production would decline rapidly, and that Americans would pay a good deal more for their food products.

This problem, then, begins with a very clear value conflict: Whereas Americans want to enjoy a high standard of living which has come about in part by the application of scientific and technological knowledge to agriculture, we also need to preserve the plants, animals, air, soil, and water from pollution and destruction by unwise use of chemicals (and other uses of technology, e.g., "soil compacting," which happens to the land when it feels the weight of a heavy tractor). Follow-up discussion might revolve around such questions as these:

What effects do chemicals used for weed or insect control have on insects, animals, bird and water life? How do we know what these effects are? Is it possible to employ more benign ways of dealing with weeds, insect pests, and plant and animal diseases, e.g., no-till agriculture, the deliberate use of predators to control insects, the breeding of disease-resistant and hardier stocks both of plants and animals? By the same token, would no-till agriculture do something good for rivers, streams and ponds which—like the Wabash River in Indiana—are turbid, muddy and polluted?

If the answer is that these are all good ideas, the next questions might be these: "What consequences would flow from this radical change in agriculture? How would it impact market prices? Investment? Research? American lifestyle? Would it make the life of many farmers economically impossible? Would it affect the agribusiness industry, especially that which produces chemicals?"

These questions cannot be rationally, empirically, and completely answered by discussion only, although discussion designed to clarify beliefs is essential. Provisional answers to these questions can only be found by research, guided inquiry, access to sources of data, and interviews with authorities and specialists, i.e., a broad knowledge base. An inquiry undertaking might well involve English teachers and librarians (or, more likely, media specialists) who would no doubt be ecstatically happy to be helpful providing information on library usage, access to electronic data, keeping records, taking notes, organizing data, etc.

THE NEW DEAL, ROOSEVELT, AND CREEPING SOCIALISM

This last illustration of reflective teaching might work well in a high-school or university classroom. Assume a course called "American History since 1865," and assume that the topic for the day is "The Great Depression" (which is, I have been told frequently, one of the two most boring subjects in American history, the other being Post-Civil-War Reconstruction). Instead of a dreary recitation of what is conventionally called the alphabet soup of the many federal agencies—the AAA, WPA, and CCC (the Agricultural Adjustment Act, the Works Progress Administration, the Civilian Conservation Corps)—the instructor poses a problem for the students, but *not* the usual uninspiring question: "What problems did Roosevelt face in 1933?" (Despite the label "problem" in that question, there is no problem because Roosevelt's problem has not yet become a problem either for the teacher or the students.) Instead, the initial question is this: "Knowing what we know today, what sort of advice would you have given Roosevelt about bank failures, unemployment, foreclosures, hunger, gloomy morale, and the estimated one million Americans who 'hopped the rails' (i.e., stowed away in railroad cars) looking for any job?"

The usual response to this question might be a litany of federalist suggestions: "The government should be the 'employer of last resort' and put the unemployed to work on useful projects; offer low-interest loans for housing; subsidize farmers; put teeth into regulation of the stock and bond market." The teacher's next ploy, then, is to ask: "But if you did all of these things, wouldn't this set up socialism, or, worse, creeping socialism?" (This question usually gets everyone's attention!) A frequently voiced complaint by Republicans since the New Deal has been that government agencies and bureaucracies set up by FDR Democrats were bad for the country for the following reasons: 1) they were an abdication of free-market economic theory, 2) they became a bloated bureaucratic monstrosity, 3) they wasted billions of dollars, 4) they established an army of decision-makers who were never elected, thereby departing from the wishes of the Founding Fathers, 5) they needlessly complicated life for everyone, who had to fill out endless forms and face bureaucratic harassment.

Students are usually caught on the horns of a dilemma. If they agree that the New-Deal Depression-relief measures brought in socialism, unmanageable bureaucracies, economic waste, overtaxation, and removed political power from state and local governments, then the next question is this: "How differently would *you* have advised President Roosevelt to deal with the miseries of the Depression?" If, on the other hand, they agree that Roosevelt did the economically right and humanly compassionate thing in 1933, then they are endorsing "creeping socialism" and all of its accompanying evils. Lacking a ready answer to this question which has distressed our society throughout the second half of the 20th century, students are likely to internalize the problem, the desired starting place for reflective inquiry. Under these circumstances, the only out is for them to reflect on the problem. Exactly what kind of problem they are identifying is not only unclear, it is unlikely to become clear. Any given problem may be phrased any way one wishes in reflective inquiry, and different students will phrase the problem differently.

Critical reflection necessarily takes them away from the usual shallow textbook treatment and towards research. Research includes reading other textbooks, looking at some of the original sources now readily available on microfiche (e.g., newspapers, magazines, journals), and interviewing elderly relatives or neighbors who lived through the Depression and remember the New Deal. Some gifted students may tackle serious scholarly research in journals of sociology, history, political science, social psychology, economics and especially on some of the paintings, cartoons, novels, poems, essays and diaries of the '30s and '40s.

This discussion of the Depression, FDR, and the New Deal is essentially a model of how to internalize a problem as a necessary step to reflective teaching, thinking, and learning. From Jack and his beanstalk to social philosophy and the Great Depression, critical thought and discourse do not begin until the students internalize a problem, and not a pseudo-problem but a real one, one that stirs up puzzlement, tension, and confusion. Students typically identify problems that cannot be conveniently fitted into any one discipline; critical reflection is essentially interdisciplinary because real problems are not the exclusive property of philosophy, literary analysis, or the social sciences. This means that evidence and analysis will not only be multidisciplinary, crossing the boundaries of differing intellectual disciplines, but also they will necessarily involve the thoughts, emotions, and wills of your students. Because real problems do involve students' feelings and wills, they depart from usual classroom content. Dealing with a problem requires a teacher who is both informed and imaginative. It takes a good deal of effort on the teacher's part to establish the problem, lead reflective discussions, assist in research, and devise effective evaluation devices.

This last observation suggests a question that all teachers who are asked to promote reflection will raise: Where does the problem come from?

The students themselves need not *propose* the problem. Problems can come from any source whatever—from the teacher during discussion, from the textbook, from newspapers and television, from events taking place in the school. The *source* of the problem is no issue; what is necessary is that students define, sense, internalize or feel the problem, and make it their own.

IMPLICATIONS OF APPLIED CRITICAL INQUIRY FOR SCHOOLS

The implications of this theory of reflective inquiry for teachers, schools, students, administrators, librarians, and others, extend in many directions. Here are a few:

SOCIAL STUDIES

A novel approach to reflective inquiry was recommended by Fredrick Ginocchio. (Ginocchio, 1986) Picking up on an incident that occurred a week before a class, Ginocchio stated baldly that skiing is a better winter activity than snowmobiling. Inundated by a torrent of enraged student reactions, Ginocchio then attempted to employ a concept from Aristotle's *Nichomachean Ethics* concerning "...how people can achieve happiness." He employed

Aristotle's definition of happiness to "prove" that skiing, which is "better physically and mentally for the individual, is more fitted to a life of virtuous work." Assuming that Ginocchio was neither deliberately indoctrinating his students in Aristotelian philosophy—a reasonable qualification, since there is abundant evidence that Aristotle lends himself easily for use as indoctrination (Wynne, 1963)—here, then, is an example of the deliberate introduction of an "anomaly," which constitutes a problem. Ginocchio concluded that his direct approach could be broadened to include "Plato on government, Thoreau on environment, or Tolstoy on patriotism and war." The point of it all:

> *It is possible to apply philosophical ideas to practical situations and have a lively classroom discussion on ethics. This lesson teaches students to remove ethical decision making from the realm of individual emotion and to put it into the realm of reason and argumentation. It teaches students that there is an objective basis for making decisions.* (Ginnochio, 1986)

BOARDS OF EDUCATION

Perhaps the most important contribution of a Board of Education is to translate its awareness of the purposes and strategies of reflective inquiry into policy. Such policy would be used to protect individual teachers who teach their students to reflect upon issues that are considered "controversial." This policy would be based on one of the many statements about academic freedom, for instance, in Indiana the statement adopted by the Indiana Council for the Social Studies, or the statement adopted by the Office of Intellectual Freedom of the American Library Association (*The American School Board Journal*). Policy in support of reflective thinking could also be translated into enlarging school library holdings, as an effort to wean teachers from their one-textbook dependency. Instead of the traditional stand-pat, conservative opposition to curriculum change, American school districts could emulate the Toronto Board of Education. In 1981, they made a statement concerning a curriculum called "Thinking and Deciding in a Nuclear Age," recognizing it as a topic that was "complex and controversial, intellectually and emotionally challenging, and rarely treated in textbooks." (Wells, 1985) Later, the Board adopted a "five-year plan, dealing with nuclear disarmament, the impact of technology on the world of work, equal rights, north/south disparities, and pollution and resource depletion." Were school-board members to support, rather than oppose, curriculum that encourages students to examine controversial issues, and to communicate their support to teachers, this would constitute the single most important and positive change in American education that one could imagine.

TEACHER IN-SERVICE TRAINING

The success of reflective inquiry depends upon the skills, insights, and willingness of teachers to implement the program. In actuality, teachers need to *un*learn before the students can begin learning. Robert Sternberg compiled a list of self-defeating assumptions held by teachers that must be addressed before they can deal with critical thought. These include the following:

❖ The defeating assumption that "the teacher is the teacher, and the student is the learner." This dichotomy is not tenable, for teachers must go through essentially the same process as do students. "Critical thinking," says Sternberg, is by no means "the students' job and only the students' job." The teacher must participate in problem sensing, must maintain an open mind, must interpret data, and, in short, must think about all aspects of a problem.

❖ The defeating assumption that any commercially produced critical-thinking program is appropriate for your school. Sternberg pointed out that commercial programs are peddled the same way that cigarettes are: They may not be appropriate to *these* students in *this* school. Not all commercial critical-thinking programs are premised on the same assumptions about the meaning and implications of inquiry. (Sternberg, 1987)

Teachers must *first* have their own conception of inquiry. (Bigge and Shermis, 1991) They must be able to translate objectives written at a high level of abstraction into something operational. They must be able to answer a variety of questions, and address a variety of issues, before they can ask administrators and school boards to lay out hard cash—usually amounting to thousands of dollars—on a commercial program. At present, computer hard- and software companies can make whatever claims they want about their products, and it is virtually impossible either to disprove or validate them.

BASAL READING TEXTS

For better or for worse, basal readers have been lodged in schools, and one cannot imagine any condition in the present in which teachers will give them up. Nevertheless, it is possible to inject inquiry into the teaching of reading even in the first grade. While basal readers are probably—as critics charge—bland, dull, based on an unconscious and unexamined middle-class, White, American conception of life, and premised upon the assumption that teachers are unimaginative technicians who need a detailed blueprint for every second of every lesson—it is nevertheless possible for teachers to go beyond the bleak array of questions in the teacher's manual. There are indeed alternative options to the usual questions, e.g., "What did Chicken Little say?" or, "What did the pig say when that deluded fowl announced that the sky is falling?"

While teachers use the Chicken Little story—or similar fables and fairy stories—to "help students build their listening skills and perhaps their vocabulary," it is possible to integrate questions "keyed to helping students consider the reliability of sources of information." (Swartz, 1986, p. 43) Such questions, for example, include these:

❖ "What made Chicken Little believe that the sky was falling?" (Translated into adult language: "What was Chicken Little's evidence that the sky was falling?")

❖ "Could something have happened that fooled Chicken Little into thinking that the sky was falling? What, for example?" (In adult language: "Can sensory evidence be misleading?")

❖ "Should we believe some people more than we believe others?" "How shall we evaluate the credentials of any witness, or indeed, anyone who makes an assertion? Why? How do you know?" That is, "What criteria does one use to decide who is, and is not, a 'reliable' witness?"

Other questions, at different levels of abstraction, can be asked. Thus, instead of the usual who, what, where, when, or why ("Why?" of course, meaning, "What does the *textbook* say?"), the teacher can use the narrative in the basal reader to ask application, analysis, synthesis, and evaluation questions, such as these:

❖ "Why did all of the animals believe Chicken Little's story?"

❖ "Is it possible to fool *everyone*?"

❖ "Have you ever been led to believe (i.e., reached a conclusion about) something that turned out to be both false and silly?"

❖ "What happened when you did?" ("What were the consequences? What are the implications of reaching unwarranted conclusions, namely, those based on false assumptions, insufficient evidence, or incorrect inferences?")

Artful questioning strategies, used carefully, can raise significant intellectual problems—that is, can introduce an "anomaly"—by reversing all the assumptions ordinarily accepted for thinking about the classic fable of Chicken Little. The point, however, is not simply to turn the story upside down. The objective is to encourage young thinkers to order their own lives through critical thinking rather than through uncritical acceptance of other people's assumptions. As the teacher, you are trying to get your students to ask themselves the following questions:

❖ "How do I go about evaluating all standards, including those accepted both publicly and tacitly and by everyone—or almost everyone—in my society?"

❖ "If I wish to reject a common standard, on what basis can I do so? What then do I substitute for the rejected value?"

These questions may then prompt students to affirm the old cliché: "When in Rome, do as the Romans do." But what if the Romans cheer murderous combats between gladiators, and applaud unspeakable cruelty to animals in the Arena? Do we adopt Roman behavior in that case?

Clever students may extrapolate from ancient Roman culture to contemporary practices, and compare Roman gladiators with TV boxers and karate experts. They may draw some relationship between animal combat in the Arena with animal experimentation in the best American universities and laboratories. Questions like these will very likely lead to discussion of topics, issues, and problems which, although they cannot be anticipated, may well prove to be fruitful, interesting, and stimulating.

SCIENCE

Judith Segal and Susan Chipman discussed learning and unlearning. Science students often fail to understand "accepted scientific theory" because they entertain misconceptions. Rather than ignoring and dismissing their misconceptions, science teachers can develop questioning strategies for eliciting misconceptions, and then use the inaccurate information itself as a basis for introducing and developing a philsophically examined approach to the problem of knowing. A responsive use of student misconceptions can generate motivation to examine their pre-scientific distorted, unfounded, or factually unsupported beliefs, and replace them with a more adequately scientific base. (Segal and Chipman, 1984, p. 86)

Research on what children understand about human anatomy and physiology has revealed a kind of wonderland of misconceptions. Especially among the very young but also among high-school and college students, misinformation abounds. Students in great numbers, kindergartners to postgraduates, lack a dependable stock of knowledge about sexual functioning, sexual physiology, conception, contraception, and abortion.

Similarly, their understanding of evolutionary theory—that most basic concept in biology, palaeontology, anthropology, and many other sciences—is usually badly garbled. This is hardly surprising, for these subjects are rarely broached by parents, and schools deal with them in only a perfunctory manner. Moreover, discussion of either topic is liable to cause a teacher to run afoul of entrenched religious orthodoxies. Ignorance notwithstanding, it is precisely because students of all ages have a distorted understanding of biological phenomena that teachers ought to include discussion of them as key components in a science curriculum, and their implications in other curricula. Student ignorance and misconceptions, combined with a keen interest in the subject, provide motivation for reflective inquiry into many biological topics in many kinds of classes.

HOME ECONOMICS

Two specialists in home economics argued that "when the problem-solving process is used within the classroom, students see all their problem-solving strategies as being in some way related rather than as isolated sets of techniques associated with a particular problem in a particular unit." (DeWald-Link and Wallace, 1983, p. 215)

They then identified the following areas in home economics as lending themselves to reflective treatment:

❖ *Controversial issues:* Abortion, the right of a woman to act autonomously concerning her body and reproductive processes, conflicts with the "sanctity of life." This illustrates an important assumption in reflective inquiry: Many problems reflect conflict between two or more cherished values. The converse is also true: Many problems reflect choices between the lesser of two evils.

❖ *Management issues:* Dual roles often make social roles in our society inherently conflictual. For example, unless women managers and administrators assert themselves, they will never be promoted, but any woman who is assertive risks being labeled as pushy, aggressive, or that most stinging of all insults, a bitch.

❖ *Consumer issues:* Credit is a serious but largely neglected area of behavior. Individuals are simultaneously told to save, borrow prudently, and never overextend their credit, but they are also sent unrequested credit cards in the mail, badgered by advertisers to purchase, and victimized by manufacturers' deliberate "planned obsolescence."

❖ *Human relations issues:* Stereotyping is an especially useful topic for reflective inquiry because adolescents entertain an immense number of unflattering stereotypes of authorities, e.g., administrators, law officers, teachers, parents, clergy, even though young people are repeatedly commanded to be respectful of, and obedient to, all these authority figures.

❖ *Nutrition issues:* Fad dieting raises questions about "ideal body types" and where young people learn about them. To this topic may also be added foods dripping with fat, cholesterol, salt, sugar and empty calories—all of which have traditionally pervaded the menus of fast-food restaurants, the kind that adolescents frequent. (Although fast-food corporate decision-makers have apparently made a real effort to follow nutritional guidelines, adolescents tend to prefer fat and sugar, they snack and avoid regular meals, and they typically make poor nutritional choices. After all, they were raised by their parents, eating what their family ate.)

❖ *Parenthood issues:* Discipline is an especially fertile field for discussion because parents—as well as teachers and students—are unable to distinguish among discipline as punishment; discipline imposed from within, i.e., self-discipline; discipline originating externally; discipline that is "too harsh"; and discipline that is "too permissive."

GIVING THE LAST WORD TO DEWEY

A century of educational reform in this society has yielded very little substantive change in teaching practices. Teachers teach now much as they did in the 19th century, although their workplace is more pleasant, classes are smaller, textbooks are cosmetically more attractive, and computers and other electronic gadgetry litter their schools. Millions of dollars spent on attempts to institute new curricula and new teaching strategies have been largely ineffectual. This is so because the assumptions held by teachers are diametrically opposed to the best suggestions arising from curriculum reform movements throughout the 20th century. A proposal to engage in reflective inquiry—or any other attempt to effect significant change in schools—will not be accepted by teachers who believe that they *must* cover textbook material because the "community" insists that this be done.

The only hope for substantial curricular reform and for adoption of reflective inquiry in American schools is for teachers to redefine the basic pedagogical concepts that they have inherited. They must substitute for self-defeating, authoritarian, and unreflective assumptions and practices an harmonious theory of critical thought that will do what John Dewey declared in 1910 to be the most crucial need in our society: that students be taught to reflect upon what they learn in schools.

Appendix

The Bloom Taxonomy: A Brief Synopsis

Introduction

"Bloom's Taxonomy, Cognitive Domain," to which I have referred several times, is an attempt to organize knowledge on a linear scale, from most concrete to most abstract. It has been in use since the mid-1960s, when Professor Benjamin Bloom of the University of Chicago directed a task force on the project. Bloom's Taxonomy, having attained the status of a convention in the field, is canonical among educationists; therefore, it makes a familiar and handy frame of reference.

Level I

Called "knowledge," Level I is concerned exclusively with memorization. A Level-I question sounds like this: When? Who? What? Where? What is the name of...? Quote the principle of.... What is the definition of "osmosis?" ...of a "transitive verb?" While a "why" question may be asked, it is often another way of asking a memory-level question, e.g., What does the text or lecture say about why a tragic hero always possesses a fatal flaw which defeats him?

Level II

Called "comprehension" or "understanding," Level II builds on Level I, but goes beyond to see if a student has grasped the tool use of a concept. Level-II questions often deal with illustrations and examples. This level asks students to cite the principle which explains *this* example. Comprehension-level questions sound like this: Can you refer to some examples of an historical revolution? What is the principal defining character of any social revolution? What makes Hamlet an example of a tragic hero?

LEVEL III

Called "application," Level III questions build on the first two levels, but introduce some element of novelty. A typical Level-III question in mathematics would deal first with the formula for finding the area of a rectangle; then it would ask, "If Sears Roebuck has a sale on carpets, in which a particular carpet sells for $25.00 a square yard, how much would it cost you to carpet your living room which is 15 feet wide and 20 feet long?" Or, an Application-level question might ask this: "Given the definition of a tragic hero that you learned yesterday, including the examples, who among modern American politicians might qualify for the title 'tragic hero'?"

LEVEL IV

Called "analysis," Level-IV questions ask students first to identify some entity, i.e., a novel, a poem, Marx's "Labor Theory of Value." It then asks them to break the entity down into component parts. Then it requires students to relate the component parts in some logical order. Finally, it asks them to put an interpretation on the result or to spell out the meaning. Analysis/Level-IV questions sound like this: "Provide a Marxian analysis of the most recent American economic recession." "Using a model of 'educational equity,' how equitable is the tax basis of Missouri's educational taxation?" "Using the text of the *Song of Songs*, describe the ways in which the author used nature metaphors to make his point about the 'eternal love triangle' between God, the people of Israel, and the land."

LEVEL V

Called "synthesis," Level V is the obverse of analysis. That is, if analysis requires one to break an entity down into its component parts, synthesis is that whole into which the components can be put together again. A typical synthesis is to be found in the last five pages of any detective novel where the Great Detective explains to his astounded hearers how he used the evidence to decide that Colonel Coffee murdered Lady Soames. Some synthesis-level questions are these: "On the basis of the archaeological evidence unearthed in the 185 B.C.E. stratum, paint a picture of this culture." "What general impressions about the painter's techniques do you receive upon analysis of Michelangelo's Sistine Chapel ceiling?" "What features characterize President Bush's conception of the 'new' (Post-Persian-Gulf-War) 'world order'?" "Given everything that you know about the landscaping requirements, budget, goals, procedures, etc., of the Wabash Valley Mental Health Center, plan, design and present a complete landscape design for the institution."

LEVEL VI

Called "evaluation," Level VI consists of two parts. Part one is "evaluation where criteria are provided." Part two is "evaluation where individuals create their own criteria." Any evaluation requires a judgment, estimate, appraisal, or assessment of some entity. As is true of all Levels from II to V, Level VI builds upon all levels below VI.

At the simplest level of judgement, any parent can ask any normal three-year-old what he or she thinks of a birthday cake, and receive an evaluation. At the most complex level, a judgment may call for an intricate interpretation and a multidimensional set of conclusions about an entire civilization.

Evaluation questions with criteria might include a beauty-queen contest where the criteria are given the judges, who then render a verdict as to the fairest of the fair. If the criteria are not spelled out, they may be devised. Criteria can be unconscious, as in a moviegoer who makes a judgment about the latest Stephen King thriller but has no articulated reasons as to why the movie is loved, rejected, despised, accepted, etc. Questioning may result in the judger becoming aware of the criteria.

Criteria may be created or devised consciously. Thus, a family wishing to buy the best possible automobile at a given price may discover that they are building criteria related to mileage, cost, average rate of repair, appearance, cargo capacity, comfort, etc.

Evaluation-level questions sound like these: "Why do so many pianists consider Vladimir Horowitz to have been the world's greatest pianist?" "What did you think of *The Red Badge of Courage?*" "What should be the punishment for the scoundrels convicted in the most recent Savings and Loan Association scandal?"

BIBLIOGRAPHY

"A Closer Look at Textbooks," *Educational Leadership*, 42 (April, 1985): 3-37.

Allen, John P. "An Analysis of Variables Related to Personality Factors and Inquiry Questioning Strategies." Doctoral dissertation, Purdue University, 1979.

Apple, Michael. *The Curriculum: Problems, Politics and Possibilities.* Albany: State University of New York Press, 1988.

Aristotle. *Metaphysics*, Book XII, in *The Works of Aristotle*, Volume I. Chicago: Encyclopedia Britannica.

Atwood, Virginia, ed. "Historical Foundations of Social Studies Education," *Journal of Thought*, 17 (Fall) 1982: 7-11.

"Australopithecus, A Long-Armed Short-Legged Knuckle Walker," *Science News*, 100 (November 27, 1971) 357.

Bar-Tal, Daniel and Leonard Saxe, eds. *Social Psychology of Education Theory and Research*. New York: John Wiley and Sons, 1978.

Barnard, J. Lynn, F.W. Carrier, Arthur William Dunn, and Clarence D. Kingsley. *The Teaching of Community Civics*. Bulletin No. 23, Washington, D.C.: Government Printing Office, 1915.

Barth, James L. and S. Samuel Shermis. "Nineteenth Century Origins of the Social Studies Movement: Understanding the Continuity between Older and Contemporary Civics and U.S. History Textbooks," *Theory and Research in Social Education*, 8 (Fall, 1980): 29-49.

Barth, James L. and S. Samuel Shermis. *Methods of Instruction in Social Studies Education*, second edition. Washington, D.C.: University Press of America.

Bayles, Ernest E. *The Theory and Practice of Teaching*. New York: Harper and Brothers, 1950.

Bayles, Ernest E. *Democratic Educational Theory*. New York: Harper and Row, 1960.

Bayles, Ernest and Bruce L. Hood. *Growth of American Educational Thought and Practice*. New York: Harper and Row, 1966.

Bayles, Ernest E. *Pragmatism in Education*. New York: Harper and Row, 1966.

Best, John Hardin and Robert T. Sidwell, eds. *The American Legacy of Learning: Readings in the History of Education*. Philadelphia: J. B. Lippincott Company, 1967.

Bigge, Morris. *Positive Relativism, An Emergent Educational Philosophy*. New York: Harper and Row, 1971.

Bigge, Morris. *Learning Theories for Teachers*, third edition. New York: Harper and Row, 1976.

Bigge, Morris L. and Maurice P. Hunt. *Psychological Foundations of Education: An Introduction to Human Development and Learning*, third edition. New York: Harper and Row, 1968.

Bigge, Morris and S. Samuel Shermis. *Learning Theories for Teachers*, fifth edition. New York: Harper Collins, 1991.

Bowers, C. A. "Educational Computing and the Ecological Crisis: Some Questions about Our Curriculum Priorities," *Journal of Curriculum Studies*, 22 (1990): 72-76.

Boydston, Jo Ann, ed. *Guide to the Works of John Dewey*. Carbondale: Southern Illinois University Press, 1970.

Brannen, Buster Duke. "An Investigation of Inquiry Questioning Strategies Used by Secondary Social Studies Teachers." Doctoral dissertation, Purdue University, 1973.

Brown, Isaac Hinton and Charles Walter Brown. *Common School Examiner and Review*. Chicago: A. Flanagan Co., 1898.

Button, H. Warren and Eugene F. Provenzano, Jr. *History of Education and Culture in America*, second edition. Englewood Cliffs, N. J.: Prentice Hall, 1989.

"Coming to Grips with the Great Textbook Machine," *Social Education, 50* (January, 1986): 39-70.

Committee of Five, *The Study of History in Secondary Schools, Report to the American Historical Association*. New York: The Macmillan Company, 1911.

"Correspondence Theory of Truth," *The Encyclopedia of Philosophy*, vol. 2. New York: The Macmillan Company, 1967.

Curti, Merle. *The Social Ideas of American Educators*, new and revised edition. Paterson, New Jersey: Littlefield, Adam and Company, 1965.

Dantonio, Marylou. "Teaching Thinking in English," *Illinois School Journal, 65* (1985): 3-9.

DeBono, Edward. "The Direct Teaching of Thinking as a Skill," *Phi Delta Kappan, 65* (June, 1983): 703-708.

Dewald-Link, Margaret R. and Sharon A. Wallace. "Students Face Tomorrow: Use Problem-Solving Approaches in Your Classroom Today," *Clearing House, 56* (January, 1983).

Dewey, John. *Democracy and Education*. New York: Macmillan Co., 1916.

Dewey, John. *The School and Society*. Chicago: University of Chicago Press, 1915.

Dewey, John. *Human Nature and Conduct*. New York: Modern Library, 1922.

Dewey, John. "Public Opinion," *The New Republic, 30* (May 3, 1922): 1,927.

Dewey, John. *The Public and Its Problems*. New York: Henry Holt, 1927.

Dewey, John. *How We Think*. Boston: D. C. Heath, 1910, revised in 1933.

Dewey, John. *Logic: The Theory of Inquiry.* New York: Henry Holt and Company, 1938.

Dewey, John. *Essays in Experimental Logic.* New York: Dover, 1953.

Dunn, Arthur William, compiler. *The Social Studies in Secondary Education,* Bulletin no. 28. Washington: United States Bureau of Education and National Association Association, 1916.

Engle, Shirley H. "Alan Griffin (1907-1964)," in Virginia Atwood, ed., *Journal of Thought,* 17 (Fall, 1982): 45-54.

Farley, John P. "The Life and Thought of Alan Griffin: Exemplar of Reflection." Doctoral dissertation, Ohio State University, 1978.

Freire, Paulo. *The Politics of Education: Culture, Power and Liberation.* South Hadley, Massachusetts: Bergin and Garvey, 1985.

Galbraith, John Kenneth. *The Affluent Society.* Boston: Houghton Mifflin, 1958.

Galbraith, John Kenneth. *The New Industrial State.* Boston: Houghton Mifflin, 1967.

Ginnochio, Frederick L. "The Question of Pleasure. Teaching Ethics in High School Social Studies," *Social Studies,* 77 (July-August, 1986): 155-157.

Goodman, Paul. *Growing Up Absurd: Problems of Youth in the Organized System.* New York: Random, 1960.

Harrington-Lueker, Donna. "Book Battles," *The American School Board Journal,* 178 (February, 1991): 18-21, 37.

Henry, Jules. *Culture against Man.* New York: Random House, 1963.

Henry, Nelson B., ed. *The Forty-First Yearbook of the National Society for the Study of Education. Part II, The Psychology of Learning.* Chicago: The University of Chicago Press, 1942.

Hilgard, Ernest R. *Theories of Learning.* New York: Appleton-Century-Crofts, 1948.

Hughes, Carolyn S. "Teaching Strategies for Developing Student Thinking," *School Library Media Quarterly,* 15 (Fall, 1986): 33-36.

Hunkins, Francis P. *Questioning Strategies and Techniques.* Boston: Allyn and Bacon, 1972.

Hullfish, H. Gordon and Philip Smith. *Reflective Thinking: The Method of Education.* New York: Dodd Mead and Company, 1961.

Hunt, Maurice P. *Foundations of Education Social and Cultural Perspectives.* New York: Holt, Rinehart and Winston, 1975.

Hutchings, John and S. Samuel Shermis. "The Origin of Age-Grading," manuscript, Purdue University, W. Lafayette, Indiana, 1991.

Immegart, Glen L. and Francis J. Pilecki. *An Introduction to Systems for the Educational Administrator.* Reading, Massachusetts: Addison-Wesley, 1973.

Jackson, Philip. *Life in Classrooms.* New York: Holt, Rinehart and Winston, 1968.

Jenkinson, Edward B. *Censorship in the Classrooms: The Mind Benders.* Carbondale, Illinois: Southern Illinois University Press, 1979.

Johnson, Donald C. and James Shreeve. *Lucy's Child: The Discovery of a Human Ancestor.* New York: Morrow, 1989.

Johnson, Earl S. "The Social Studies versus the Social Sciences," in Metcalf, Lawrence E., John DeBoer, Walter V. Kaulfers, *Secondary Education. A Textbook of Readings.* Boston: Allyn and Bacon, 1966.

Jowett, Benjamin, trans. *Plato's The Republic.* New York: The Modern Library, no date.

Karier, Clarence. *Man, Society, and Education: A History of American Educational Ideas.* Glenview, Illinois: Scott, Foresman and Company, 1967.

Katz, Michael B. *Class, Bureaucracy and Schools, The Illusion of Educational Change in America,* expanded edition. New York: Praeger Publishers, 1975.

Kurfis, Joanne G. *Critical Thinking: Theory, Research, Practice and Possibilities.* ASHE-ERIC Higher Education Report No. 2, Washington, D. C.: Association for the Study of Higher Education, 1988.

Laudan, Larry. *Science and Relativism. Some Key Controversies in the Philosophy of Science.* Chicago: University of Chicago Press, 1990.

Leakey, Richard E. and Roger Lewin. *Origins: What New Discoveries Reveal about the Emergence of Our Species and Its Possible Future.* New York: Dutton, 1973.

Leavitt, Harold J. *et al. The Social Science of Organizations: Four Perspectives.* New York: Harcourt, Brace, and Jovanovich.

Mandinach, Ellen B. and Marcia C. Linn. "The Cognitive Effects of Computer Learning Environments," *Journal of Education Computing Research,* 2 (1986): 411-427.

McLuhan, Marshall, Kathryn Hutchon, Eric McLuhan. *Media, Messages & Language: The World as Your Classroom.* Skokie, Illinois: National Textbook Co., 1980.

Metcalf, Lawrence, John J. DeBoer, Walter V. Kaulfers. *Secondary Education: A Textbook of Readings.* Boston: Allyn and Bacon, 1966.

Millstein, Mike M. and James A. Belasco. *Educational Administration and the Behavioral Sciences: A Systems Perspective.* Boston: Allyn and Bacon, 1973.

Moses, Monte and Jan Thomas. "Teaching Students to Think— What Can Principals Do?" *National Association of Secondary School Principals,* 70 (March, 1986): 16-20.

Neilsen, Allan R. *Critical Thinking and Reading: Empowering Learners to Think and Act.* Bloomington, Indiana: ERIC Clearinghouse on Reading and Communication Skills and Urbana, Illinois: National Council of Teachers of English, 1989.

Newmann, Fred M. "Introduction," *National Center on Effective Secondary Schools Newsletter, 2* (Spring, 1987): 1.

Parramore, Barbara M. "The Role of the Textbook in the Curriculum: Past, Present and Future," National Council for the Social Studies, November 23, 1985.

Pratte, Richard. *Pluralism in Education: Conflict, Clarity and Commitment.* Springfield, Illinois: Thomas, 1979.

Pratte, Richard. *The Public School Movement: A Critical Study.* New York: McKay, 1973.

Raths, Louis, Arthur Jonas, Arnold Rothstein, Selma Wassermann. *Teaching for Thinking Theory and Application.* Columbus, Ohio: Charles E. Merrill, 1967.

"Reforming College Sports: How? When? Ever?" *Academe, 77* (January-February, 1991).

Schultz, Stanley. *The Culture Factory.* New York: Oxford University Press, 1973.

Segal, Judith W. and Susan Chipman. "Thinking and Learning Skills: The Contribution of the National Institute of Education," *Educational Leadership, 46* (September, 1984): 85-87.

Shermis, Samuel. "Interaction in the Writings of John Dewey." M.A. thesis, University of Kansas, Lawrence, Kansas, 1960.

Shermis, S. Samuel and James L. Barth. "Problem Definition, Problem-Solving and Social Problems: Reconceptualizing the Thought Process in Philosophy," *Journal of Thought, 18* (Winter, 1983): 73-93.

Shermis, S. Samuel. "John Dewey's Social and Political Philosophy: Its Implications for Social Studies Education." Doctoral dissertation, University of Kansas, Lawrence, Kansas, 1961.

Shermis, S. Samuel. *Philosophic Foundations of Education.* New York: American Book Company, 1967.

Shermis, S. Samuel and James L. Barth. "Social Studies and the Problem of Knowledge: A Re-Examination of Edgar Bruce Wesley's Classic Definition of the Social Studies," *Theory and Research in Social Education, 55* (1978): 31-43.

Shermis, S. Samuel and James L. Barth. "We All Know What a Problem Is, Don't We?" *Peabody Journal of Education, 55* (April, 1978): 287-297.

Shermis, S. Samuel and James L. Barth. "Teaching for Passive Citizenship: A Critique of Philosophical Assumptions," *Theory and Research in Social Education, 10* (Winter, 1982): 73-93.

Siegel, Marjorie and Robert F. Carey. *Critical Thinking: A Semiotic Perspective.* Bloomington, Indiana: ERIC Clearinghouse on Reading and Communication Skills, and Urbana, Illinois: National Council of Teachers of English, 1989.

Skinner, B. F. *Cumulative Record: A Selection of Papers,* third edition. New York: Appleton-Century Crofts, 1972.

Smith, Carl B. *A Commitment to Critical Thinking.* Bloomington, Indiana: Grayson Bernard Publishers, 1991.

Snygg, Donald and Arthur W. Combs. *Individual Behavior. A New Frame of Reference for Psychology.* New York: Harper and Row, 1959.

"Social Studies: Old Masters and Founders," *The International Journal of Social Education, 3* (Winter, 1988-1989).

Spring, Joel. *The Sorting Machine Revisited: National Educational Policy since 1945,* updated edition. New York: Longman, 1989.

Spring, Joel. *Conflict of Interests. The Politics of American Education.* New York: Longman, 1988.

Spring, Joel. *American Education. An Introduction to Social and Political Aspects,* fourth edition. New York: Longman, 1989.

Stanley, William B. ed. *Review of Reearch in Social Studies Education: 1976-1983.* Bulletin 75, Boulder, Colorado: ERIC Clearinghouse for Social Studies/Social Science Education, Washington, D. C.: National Council for the Social Studies, and Boulder: Social Science Education Consortium, 1985.

Sternberg, Robert. "Teaching Critical Thinking: Eight Easy Ways to Fail before You Begin," *Phi Delta Kappan, 68* (February, 1987): 56-59.

Swartz, Robert J. "Restructuring Curriculum for Critical Thinking," *Educational Leadership, 43* (May, 1986): 43-44.

"Two Distinct Hominoids?" *Science News, 99* (June, 12, 1971): 398.

U.S.A. Today, August 9, 1989.

Woodward, Arthur. "Are We Getting Our Money's Worth from Textbooks?" Textbook Reform Conference, National Association of State Boards of Education and the Council of Chief State School Officers, Washington, D. C., June 21, 1985.

Wells, Margaret. "Peace Education in the Toronto Board of Education," *History and Social Science Teacher, 20* (Spring, 1985): 53-56.

Wiener, Philip P. *Evolution and the Founders of Pragmatism.* New York: Harper and Row, 1949.

Wolman, Benjamin B. *Contemporary Theories and Systems in Psychology.* New York: Harper and Brothers, 1960.

Wynne, John. *Theories of Education.* New York: Harper and Row, 1963.

Do You Have An Idea to Share?

Research to Report?

A Cause to Champion?

This excellent book was published by the ERIC Clearinghouse on Reading and the Communication Skills, a unit within the U.S. Department of Education's farflung network of information processing for everyone interested in education.

At ERIC/RCS, we are always looking for high-quality manuscripts having to do with teaching English, the language arts, reading, writing, speech, theater, mass communication, the media, personal communication, thinking, literature, and literacy. We publish original research and scholarship, teaching guides and practical applications for educators and others who work with youth. In conjunction with EDINFO Press and our other partners in education information, we publish books of all kinds within the field of education.

Do you have a novel understanding of some timely issue, an innovative approach to a troubling problem, or an especially effective method of teaching? Does one of your colleagues have something burning to say on curriculum development, professionalism in education, excellence in teaching, or some other aspect of schooling? If so, let us know. We'd like to hear from you. Tell us that reading this book gave you an incentive to get in touch.

Contact:

Warren Lewis
Assistant Director, Publications
ERIC/RCS
Smith Research Center, Suite 150
Bloomington, IN 47408-2698
812/855-5847
BITNET% WWLEWIS@IUBACS

OTHER TITLES FROM ERIC/RCS

Apply *critical thinking* to reading.
Promote *critical thinking* in the classroom.
Foster *critical thinking* as shared learning.

Carl Smith, in *A Commitment to Critical Thinking*, takes a wry look at a cant phrase, turns it inside out, and makes something philosophic-sounding and elitist into a highly practical, down-to-earth approach to being rationally thoughtful. He especially applies **critical thinking** techniques to foster **critical reading.**

Smith shows you how to be a Socrates with both younger and older students by asking provocative questions. Through critical thinking, younger children's run-away imaginations can be artfully directed through their fantasy to an awareness of reality. Older students respond to a variety of sophisticated techniques:

- ❖ the "art of questioning"
- ❖ discriminating between fact and opinion
- ❖ judging an author's competence
- ❖ determining an author's purpose
- ❖ recognizing propaganda techniques

Professor of Education at Indiana University, and Director of ERIC/RCS (Educational Resources Information Center, the Clearinghouse on Reading and Communication Skills), Smith equips you with the following tools to promote critical thinking in the reading classroom:

- ❖ an anticipation-reaction guide
- ❖ a structured text preview
- ❖ a three-level study guide that combines the techniques of "close reading," "historical-critical," and "reader response" approaches to interpretation

More than a how-to book, *A Commitment to Critical Thinking* presents the full range of definitions of critical thinking, and is a discussion of the changing philosophies about critical thinking. Smith makes the complex handy, and the elusive accessible.

$9.95

The **ERIC/NCTE Series on Critical Thinking** roots and grounds the language-arts teacher solidly in an intellectual tradition that upholds schoolteaching as an endeavor to hone young minds to a keen edge. Series introduction by Jerome Harste.

Critical Thinking: A Semiotic Perspective, by Margorie Siegel and Robert F. Carey, draws on the thought of C. S. Peirce to redefine critical inquiry in the classroom in terms of semiosis, the collaborative work of making meaning out of the signs of language.

Critical Thinking and Reading: Empowering Learners to Think and Act, by Allan R. Neilsen, draws on the thought of John Dewey to focus the entire learning process as a critical endeavor of the learner's own thinking, reading, and doing.

Critical Thinking and Writing: Reclaiming the Essay, by Thomas Newkirk, draws on the thought of Michel de Montaigne to breathe new life into writing the school essay by putting that well-known exercise at the service of the student essayist's own critical reflection.

$8.95 each

ERIC/RCS Special Collection #3: Critical Thinking

All the *Digests* and *FAST Bibs* from ERIC/RCS on Critical Thinking. Includes the following:

Judith Langer, "A New Look at Literature Instruction"

Charles Suhor, "Semiotics and the English Language Arts"

Marino Alvarez and Victoria Risko, "S chema Activation, Construction, and Application"

Nola Aiex, "How to 'Read' Television: Teaching Students to View TV Critically"

Carrol Tama, "Critical Thinking: Promoting It in the Classroom"

Charles Suhor, "Thinking Skills in English—and across the Curriculum"

Sally Standiford, "Metacomprehension"

Donald Lazere, "Critical Thinking in College English Studies"

Gail Londergan, "Creativity"

Michael Shermis, "Critical Reading and Thinking: Instructional Strategies"

Ruth Eppele, "Left Brain/Right Brain: Research and Learning"

...and more.

$7.95

Ship to:

Name _____

Address _____

_____

City_____State_____ ZIP _____

Phone (_____) _____

Item No.	Quantity	Abbreviated Title	Price	Total Cost
			$	
			$	
			$	
			$	
Minimum order $5.00			Subtotal	
			Plus Postage and Handling	
			TOTAL Purchase	

Method of Payment

❏ check   ❏ money order

❏ P.O. # _____

❏ MasterCard   ❏ VISA

cardholder _____

card no. _____

expiration date_____

Make checks payable to ERIC/RCS.

Order Subtotal	Postage/Handling
$5.00 - $10.00	$2.00
$10.01 - $25.00	$3.00
$25.01 - $50.00	$4.00
$50.01 - $75.00	$5.00
$75.01 - $100.00	$6.00
$100.01 - $125.00	$7.00
$125.01 - $150.00	$8.00
over $150.00	$9.00

Send order form to:
ERIC/RCS
Indiana University
2805 E. 10th Street, Suite 150E
Bloomington, IN 47408-2698
FAX (812) 855-7901

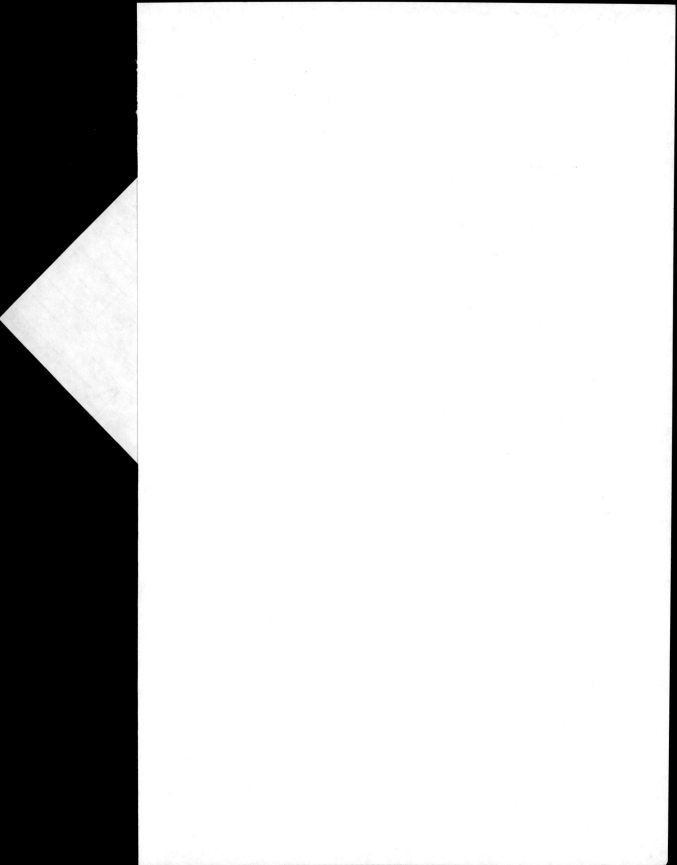

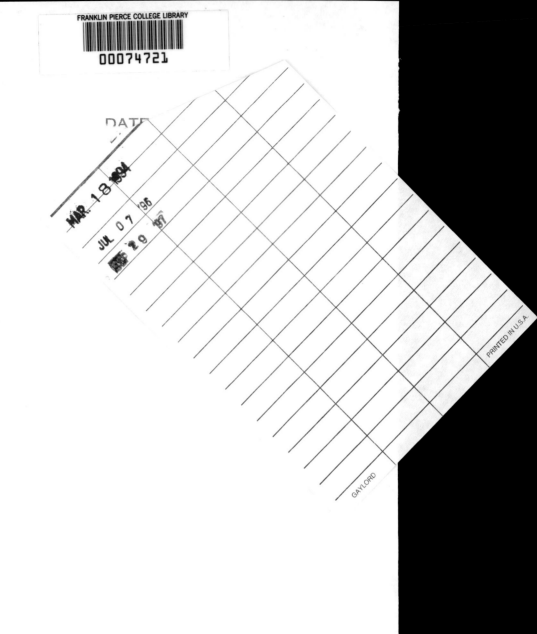